There have been a number of books written on this subject, but none that I have read that provide such clarity on servant leadership. Larry O'Donnell has provided excellent examples from his amazing career and practical applications from Scripture. Christ set the example for how we are to engage with all people, even those who aren't so easy to engage with. One of my takeaways is that servant leadership is not just for the office; it's about our entire life. It's not mechanical; it's a genuine heart toward all. Read and embrace this servant leadership approach and see your life and those around you blossom.

TOM MORGAN
Retired CEO & Chairman, Baker & Taylor
(Charlotte, North Carolina)
Retired CEO, Hughes Supply (Atlanta, Georgia)

An extraordinary read that will resonate long after you put it down. Larry O'Donnell weaves his inspirational personal story, his successful professional journey, and his deep spiritual beliefs to present a compelling case for servant leadership. For those who struggle with how to bring faith to the workplace, here is your handbook.

DENNY SLAGLE
Retired Executive Vice President, Volvo Group
Retired President, Mack Trucks (also another "Undercover Boss"; Charleston, South Carolina)

Larry O'Donnell boils down leadership to five easy-to-remember characteristics that can make anyone lead in a more powerful way. He's got credibility from his experience at Waste Management and his view that his daughter, son, wife and faith have made him the leader he is today. No one leads effectively alone!

MARK EDMUNDS
Leadership Coach
Retired Vice Chairman, Deloitte, LLP (Austin, Texas)

Life, Leadership and God—Larry O'Donnell weaves it all together in a must-read book every business leader who cares about their legacy should embrace.

JACK MOORE
Retired CEO & Chairman, Cameron International Corp. (Houston, Texas)

In today's corporate world, "servant leadership" has become a rare leadership trait indeed. The reasons are many, including the numerous distractions and heavy pressures on today's CEO, the singular focus on driving shareholder returns, the short-term nature of the CEO job, and the narrow investment time-horizon, and even the secular nature of corporate America. Larry O'Donnell does an excellent job discussing how applying those leadership skills that Christ put to work two thousand years ago can truly resonate with those people who drive the greatest value for your company . . . your hard-working employees.

JIM FISH
CEO, Waste Management (Houston, Texas)

With so much *Management Waste* in the world today, it is refreshing to hear from a true servant leader/CEO who operates with the ultimate "Undercover Boss" at the helm of his life. This is a must read for any potential or current leader who wants to know how to flip the triangle from top down to bottom up. Larry O'Donnell is a true friend, amazing husband, and extraordinary father.

RICHARD ELLIS
Senior Pastor, Reunion Church (Dallas, Texas)

Larry O'Donnell's sterling reputation as a business leader is unquestionable. What many may not know about Larry are the personal qualities he faithfully exhibits on a consistent basis day in and day out. Over the many years I've known

Larry, he has always proved to give wise counsel and can be trusted as a loving, kind, thoughtful, and generous friend with a servant heart.

MIKE HALL
President, Ron Carter Auto Group (Houston, Texas)

It's been said that if you aim at nothing, you'll hit it every time. But, Larry O'Donnell has taken strategic aim and hit the bull's-eye on servant leadership! *Management Waste* is a blueprint for personal life development in every aspect and relationship of life; leadership in the family, leadership in the workplace, and leadership in the world. But, it's much more than that— IT'S THE PLAN TO CHANGE THE PLANET!!!

DR. JOHN TOLSON
Founder of The Gathering/USA & former Team Chaplain of the Houston Rockets, Houston Astros, Houston Oilers, Orlando Magic, and Dallas Cowboys (Dallas, Texas)

Larry O'Donnell presents a strategy that benefits leaders of all organizational sizes. What makes this book so special is that it isn't complex. Larry speaks to a military man's heart by using simple acronyms that remind us to be servant leaders from the boardroom to the breakroom. Larry's illustrations from being a hands-on CEO reveal how theory becomes practice. He challenges every leader to look inside and ask, "What is motivating me?" If you are a leader, you need to read this book. Or even more directly, those you supervise need you to read this book.

CHRIS PLEKENPOL
Lead Pastor, Wells Branch Community Church
Combat Company Commander Operation Iraqi Freedom (2004–2005)
Army Ranger & Bronze Star Recipient (Austin, Texas)

Can you live out your faith as an executive in the business world? The answer is a resounding YES, and Larry O'Donnell's book *Management Waste* is a clear blueprint for how to guide an organization with solid Christian business principles. Larry's servant leadership model, outlined in this book, provides essential skills for uplifting a team that no manager should miss. Through stories of achievement and failure, blessing and tragedy, Larry has given insight into simple yet proven steps for anyone who wants to overcome *waste* in *management* and be the positive influencer in driving success.

TERRY MERTINK
Office of the President, Focus on the Family
(Colorado Springs, Colorado)

Throughout his business career, Larry O'Donnell worked hard to model a servant leader, who put the interests of others, including employees, customers, and family ahead of his own. In *Management Waste*, he is open and honest in sharing some successful examples and some not so successful examples of how to be a servant leader. *Management Waste* is a great roadmap of how to hone your servant leadership skills in a secular business world and not sacrifice your faith in God.

BRAD TUCKER
Chairman & CEO, Mustang CAT (Houston, Texas)

Management Waste: 5 Steps to Clean Up the Mess and Lead with Purpose is exactly what it claims to be: a fresh look at God's design for leadership. But this fresh look is based on an old, oft-forgotten call to a different form of governance—servant leadership. Through personal and sometimes shocking stories, Larry O'Donnell reflects on key characteristics modeled by Jesus, the Master Servant Leader. But be on guard. O'Donnell will challenge you to address your own trash and manage your personal waste! Because that's what it takes to be a game-changing leader.

MARK YARBROUGH
President, Dallas Theological Seminary (Dallas, Texas)

MANAGEMENT
WASTE

STEPS TO
CLEAN UP THE MESS
AND LEAD WITH PURPOSE

LARRY O'DONNELL III

Former President of Waste Management and Featured on the
Premiere Episode of the Hit Television Series **UNDERCOVER BOSS**

Servant Ministries Foundation
Austin, Texas

ISBN: 978-1-952421-10-5 (Print)
ISBN: 978-1-952421-14-3 (eBook)
Audio book also available

Some of the anecdotal illustrations used in this book are true to life and are included with the permission of the persons mentioned. All other illustrations are composites of real situations, and any resemblance to people living or dead is purely coincidental. For permission to reuse any content, contact Larry O'Donnell at larry@larryodonnell.com.

All Scripture quotations, unless otherwise indicated, are taken from the Holy Bible, New International Version®, NIV® Copyright © 1973, 1978, 1984, 2011 by Biblica, Inc.® Used by permission.

Scripture quotations marked ESV are taken from The Holy Bible, English Standard Version. ESV® Text Edition: 2016. Copyright © 2001 by Crossway Bibles, a publishing ministry of Good News Publishers. Used by permission.

Scripture quotations marked NASB are taken from the New American Standard Bible Copyright © 1960, 1962, 1963, 1968, 1971, 1972, 1973, 1975, 1977, 1995 by The Lockman Foundation. Used by permission.

Library of Congress Control Number: 2020918235

Printed in the United States of America

27 26 25 24 23 22 21 20   1 2 3 4 5

DEDICATION

This book is dedicated to my beautiful wife, Dare,

who is the greatest gift God has given to me other than His Son Jesus Christ. Dare has always been there for me with encouragement, constant support, love, friendship, and kindness. I would not have wanted to go through life without her, and she is a constant reminder to me of what God intended as a true servant of the Most High God. Thank you for being my best friend, always seeing the best in me, and clearly overlooking my many, many flaws.

Contents

Foreword

IT WAS 2005, and I was four years into my current nine-teen-year career at Waste Management. I was considering leaving the company because I hadn't been able to convince the leadership team that I was capable of leading one of our field operations. I mean, why couldn't I lead a team of drivers, landfill operators, and recycle sorters? I had managed financial analysts for years. "I'm smart enough to understand our operations," I told myself. But before I turned in my notice, I would place one last call to our president, Larry O'Donnell.

I didn't know Larry very well, but he had a reputation for being approachable. I had seen that firsthand when I happened to sit next to him on a Southwest Airlines flight. He had offered me a ride to my meeting that day before he drove on to his meeting. You see, I was a guy who had grown up subscribing to the Golden Rule, "Do unto others as you would have them do unto you," and Larry seemed to epitomize that. My mom was a strong Christian woman, and she preached that Golden Rule to us as kids. But for some reason, that seemed to be missing in much of corporate America.

Typically, a phone call from a low-level analyst to a senior officer at Waste Management could go for days or weeks without being returned. You could expect to hear back from the administrative assistant, but some officers wouldn't take the time to call you back themselves. Someone once said to me about one of our senior officers, "If you don't add value to him, don't expect to hear from him." Well, not Larry O'Donnell. Larry called me back within two hours. I won't ever forget that conversation as I stood in an airport terminal listening to Larry's questions and then trying to honestly answer them, so as to not ruin my chances of getting out into the field. But Larry's questions were so different from the other questions I had been asked as I looked into this possible move into field operations.

He told me, "Jim, nobody questions your intellect or your analytical abilities. But let me ask you a couple of questions. First, why do you want to make this move?"

This was a simple question in my mind, "Because I need operating experience to further my career." Of course, I cleaned it up a bit before I answered Larry. But it didn't matter.

After listening to my answer, he said, "Jim, you realize that if you are going to be successful, this job in the field isn't about you. It's about your team. It's about how they respond to you as a leader. If a sergeant can't motivate his troops to fight for him, he won't win any battles, and he sure won't ever make colonel, let alone general."

Larry's questions weren't at all about my career aspirations. They were about things like accountability and communication style. He asked me, "Jim, if your area has high driver turnover, how would you address that?"

My answer was, "I would first look at whether our pay and benefits were competitive."

Knowing Larry like I know him today, I'm sure what was running through his mind was "Wrong answer!" But instead of blurting that out, he told me a story about one of our district managers who, at the time, had the lowest employee turnover in the company. He told me that every single Thanksgiving, this manager invited a driver and his/her family over to the house to say grace over a big meal and to enjoy some football and family time. And Larry told me, "Jim, that's how you address turnover." To this day, that district manager has one of the lowest turnover numbers in the entire company. If you are fortunate enough to have a conversation like the one I had with Larry that day, you should consider yourself blessed. I truly learned more about leadership in ten minutes than I had in my previous fifteen years in business. It was a life lesson for me.

Looking back years later, I realized that what Larry was really talking about that day on the phone was servant leadership. In today's world of huge companies, disconnected CEOs and executive teams, and unhappy, dissatisfied workers, there is a real shortage of servant leadership. CEO performance goals are metrics like total shareholder returns, margin improvement, free cash flow, EBITDA (earnings before interest, taxes, depreciation, and amortization), and EPS (earnings per share) growth, etc. There is hardly a peep in those goals about improving the lives of the tens of thousands of people who ultimately report up to that CEO. And it's probably no coincidence that, in addition to CEOs being focused on wealth generation, there is also a real shortage of faith-based leaders in today's large corporations.

Even if you are a person of faith, you don't dare talk about it at work. Today's CEOs seem to believe that leadership is about providing financial rewards to those in the rank and file. And by doing so, those folks will be loyal employees. Unfortunately, that model has a limited life span. Don't misunderstand me, compensation is important. But people don't leave companies because of pay and benefits. They leave because they aren't valued, their opinions don't matter, they are dispensable, and they don't respect their leader.

Larry is one of the few who, though the servant leadership approach to leading his team, was always more interested in their well-being than his own personal financial statement. Yet ironically, when put in that order—the people first, then himself—the results were incredible. Larry is a man of action and a man of relationships who is amazingly self-aware. His adoption of the leadership principles that Christ practiced thousands of years ago is what made Larry the highly successful leader that he is. The true cornerstone of successful companies over the long-term has always been, and will always be, great leadership. And placing yourself at the service of your people, even as a CEO, is the most tried-and-true management style of all time. Christ practiced it over and over, and it seems to have worked pretty well for Him.

The interesting part of the Waste Management *Undercover Boss* episode was not that Larry worked in the field without being noticed. It wasn't even that, after the fact, he took care of the handful of WM employees with whom he interacted during the show. The interesting part about that Waste Management episode of *Undercover Boss* was how Larry used that television program to show the thousands of directors, managers, and supervisors within WM—and probably at other companies as well—what servant leadership truly is. Sure, he changed those employees' lives. But he also demonstrated, on national TV, the profound impact that putting people first in a Christlike way can have on an entire company. He showed that dedicating yourself to serving your people, not having them serve you, is the recipe for greatness in all companies, big and small. With it your employees will follow you anywhere, accomplish amazing things for your business, delight your customers, and reward your shareholders for the long-term. Without it we are all just *management waste.*

> Jim Fish
> CEO, Waste Management
> August 2020

Acknowledgments
and Disclaimer

I HAVE included many personal stories throughout this book, so I need to provide a bit of a disclaimer. Some people will remember some of the stories in this book differently from what I have described, and I expect that. So let me be clear: the stories I have included in this book are based on the facts as best as I can recall (which is getting more difficult with each passing day at this point in my life since some of the stories go back decades).

In some cases I have changed the story slightly from the way I remember it either to illustrate a point or to change the name of the character of the story or some of the details so as to not to embarrass or identify others, or for other reasons I felt were appropriate for the purposes of this book. It is absolutely not my intent to divulge any confidential, proprietary, or sensitive information of others or to embarrass or disparage anyone in any way.

I am disappointed I am not able to use the pages of this book to thank each and every colleague and friend by name who helped me throughout my career or who contributed greatly to the successes of the many teams I was on throughout my career. I hope each of you who may be reading this book and who worked with me during my career already know how much I appreciate you and understand this book is about servant leadership and bringing glory to God, not us. Therefore, in an effort not to offend or disappoint anyone, or inadvertently leave anyone out, I have only used the actual names of former colleagues who are now deceased to honor them, or people who appeared with me on the *Undercover Boss* show, since their names can be readily ascertained.

This book is not written as a true history of Waste Management or any other company I have worked for, and it is not written as a true background piece on the making of the *Undercover Boss* show. You should not rely on the accuracy of any of the stories in this book, other than the stories directly from the Bible. So, if you worked with me and recall the stories differently, please don't write me and tell me I got some of the stories wrong. Just enjoy the story, reflect on the story the way you remember it, and then apply the story to whatever point I am making in the book. The purpose of the stories I have included is to illustrate an aspect of servant leadership and to provide an analogy to help you apply the concepts of servant leadership in your own life, hopefully better than I was able to do, trying to learn how to be a servant leader as I progressed along in my own career.

I also want to briefly thank everyone who has helped me make the publishing of this, my first ever book, a reality.

First, I want to thank my wife, Dare, who without her encouragement and loving support, I would probably not have made many of the career changes discussed in this book. She was there to encourage me with tremendous grace, even though the changes always meant a more difficult life on her as I embarked on the challenges and demands of a new career path every ten years or so. Without Dare's encouragement, many of the stories told in this book would not have happened. Clearly, God has worked through Dare in many ways to help me grow in my own personal relationship with God.

To my beautiful special-needs daughter, Linley, and my son, Larry IV. Linley's tragedy told in this book has impacted all of us, but God has used the storm in a positive way for all of us. Thank you, Linley, for the positive impact you have had in my life, and thank you, Larry, for your patience with me and being such a great and empathetic son through all we have been through together with Linley. You have both been and continue to be an inspiration to me, and I am so proud to be your dad. I hope this book can be a source of inspiration and encouragement to my future grandkids (still waiting) and descendants beyond as they pursue the life God intends for them long after I have gone to join the Lord in heaven.

To my mom and dad, thank you for raising me in a Christian family and for all the love and sacrifice you have shown me throughout my life. And thank you, Dad, for teaching me the values of hard work, integrity, and appreciation for the frontline workers who do the tough jobs every day.

To my dear friend and mentor, Pastor Richard Ellis, who was the first to inspire me to write this book, and who has been a constant source of guidance, mentoring, and encouragement. Thank you for all the suggestions and creativity you provided to me as I wrote the book, as well as the help in connecting me to the right team to help me along this journey. Thank you for the faith and confidence you constantly extend to me. God truly blessed me when he put you in my life, and I will be forever grateful for your friendship.

To Mark Yarbrough, who I first got to know as one of my professors at Dallas Theological Seminary and who is now my friend and president of DTS, thank you for providing the teaching and coaching that energized my faith and put me on this new career path of ministry. I can't thank you enough for your support and your encouragement to write this book, and most of all for your friendship.

To all the team at A. Larry Ross Communications (Larry Ross, Kristin Cole, Katie Martin, Angelica Jackson, and Karoline Chapman), who have been a driving force to help guide me through the process, and who have assisted me tremendously with marketing, public relations, and social media.

To Wes Yoder, for his wisdom, coaching, editing suggestions, and publishing expertise.

To Andrea Lucado, who worked tirelessly with me on several rounds of editing that led to a much better organization of the story line and a more readable book than I could have ever done without her suggestions.

And a big thank you to my dear friend, Pastor Chris Plekenpol, who introduced me to Andrea. Thank you for your continuing encouragement to me and your friendship.

To all those who read my manuscript and provided me helpful insights into how the story line flowed, including Dare (she helped me remember many details I had forgotten), my dad, my mother-in-law Grace and father-in-law John (God blessed me with the best in-laws in the world), and Richard Ellis. And a big thank you to each of you who read the manuscript and were willing to write an endorsement for the book, and especially my friend Jim Fish, whose words in his foreword to this book brought tears to my eyes when I read it for the first time. I will be forever grateful to each of you for your kind words!

To all those who helped me in the final publishing stages of the book such as interior book design and typesetting (Lisa Parnell), copy editing (Judi Hayes), cover design (Bruce Gore), and publishing and distribution (Ryan Sprenger, Abigail Taylor, and the NewType Team).

And to all my dear friends who have been so instrumental throughout my life in leading me and discipling me to a closer relationship with our Lord. I would still be lost had it not been for your leading me to Christ, discipling me along the way, and helping me stay on the right path.

And finally, to the greatest God that could ever be, who has blessed my life beyond even my own imagination. Thank You for taking the tragedy with our daughter and using it in such a powerful and positive way in my life.

"Whoever wants to become great among you must be your servant, and whoever wants to be first must be your slave."

MATTHEW 20:26–27

CHAPTER 1

Why *Management Waste?*

Introduction

I LOVED being in business management. It is exciting, with each day bringing unexpected challenges and opportunities. One of the biggest challenges I ever had in my career was when I was recruited by Waste Management to help lead the turnaround of the company after it fell into deep trouble.

Waste Management was the largest public company blowup in history at the time (only to be followed by others like Enron and WorldCom). Waste Management averaged buying about a company a day for the year and a half before I arrived. The businesses had not been integrated, the leadership (before I arrived) started playing around with the accounting, and unfortunately, most of the senior leaders sold their stock just before the company reported they would fall tremendously short of their quarterly earnings expectations. The board of directors fired all the senior management, took over running the company, and began to look for new leadership.

Waste Management was involved in class-action lawsuits and SEC investigations, most of the former management was accused of insider trading, and the stock plummeted from the mid-$60 per share range and was trading around $13 per share on the day I arrived.

Needless to say, it was a huge mess when I got there. Each day presented us new and unexpected challenges as we began our work to get Waste Management out of the ditch and back on the road to success. Even though it was a public company generating over $13.5 billion in annual revenues, it was more like a $13.5 billion start-up company! We brought in more than a thousand accountants just to help us sort out the accounting to get the books closed. I had thick dark hair when I first started at Waste Management! Now, thanks to all the stress, I have very little hair left on top of my head, but I treat each one I have left with love and care when I brush my hair each morning! My wife cracks up laughing every morning she sees me brushing my head with no hair!

We needed to fix many problems at Waste Management. Waste Management had acquired more than twelve hundred companies around the world, resulting in many different operating models, financial systems, and cultures. We knew we needed to prioritize and focus on the critical few things we could control that would have the biggest impact first, as well as help us stabilize the company, restore integrity, and regain the trust of the employees, customers, shareholders, and regulators.

As you might imagine, it took years to sort things out at Waste Management and to develop the operating model for the company that formed the basis of what is still being used to operate the company today. I learned a lot during my ten and a half years at Waste Management, not only about what it takes to develop a high-performing and engaged team but also about how important it is to be a servant leader.

Many books have been written about servant leadership, perhaps because our culture conditions us *not* to be servant leaders. We need to be reminded of what servant leadership looks like and why we should seek to emulate it. I want to share with you some of the practical insights I have learned as I have strived to practice servant leadership throughout my decades-long career in business. I will be the first to tell you I haven't always gotten it right, and I have learned a lot from both our successes as a team and through my own personal failures along the way.

I think the opposite of servant leadership is *management waste*. What comes to your mind when you hear "management waste"? Perhaps wasted opportunities, wasted time, wasted gifts, or wasted lives. I think it encompasses all of those when we don't use the leadership principles God has provided for us. What I learned during my business career showed me what great things can happen when the principles of servant leadership are used, and what a waste it is when they are not—*management waste*!

To give you some background, I graduated from college with my engineering degree and then went to law school. But my plan was always to run my own business, not practice law. At the beginning of my career, I believed with hard work and proper planning, anything could be achieved. Early in my career I was achieving successes as I began moving up the leadership ladder. (At the time I thought it was in large part due to my own effort!) I made partner at my law firm at an early age, and I practiced law for about ten years (primarily business transactions, mergers, acquisitions, real estate, finance, and securities law).

I knew I enjoyed business more than law, so I left my law firm to become a vice president at Baker Hughes, which at the time, was the third largest oil and gas services company in the world. I was blessed to have an outstanding mentor named Jim Woods, who was the chairman and CEO of Baker Hughes when I joined. Jim taught me a lot about business and leadership. Jim continued to be one of my business mentors for decades until he passed away in 2017. I will be forever grateful for what Jim taught me and the confidence he placed in me when he promoted me to executive leadership early in my career.

I met my wife, Dare, while we were in college at the University of Texas. We married in 1981, about a year after we graduated. My wife has been the biggest blessing and gift God has given to me outside of the gift of His Son. We have two children: our daughter Linley, born in 1985, and our son Larry IV, born in 1989. He is married to our beautiful daughter-in-law Christina. This is our family today, but there was a time when I didn't think our family would look like this.

Our Shipwreck

When Dare and I were about to have our first child, I was feeling pretty good about myself as a person, husband, and young leader, and I was excited with the thought of becoming a father. I became a Christian at a youth group retreat when I was a teenager. Before the retreat I felt like I was a hopeless sinner. When I placed my faith in Jesus Christ, I experienced an incredible sense of peace and comfort knowing my sins are now forgiven and He has promised me eternal life with Him. God tells us that, even though we become Christians, we are to expect to face difficult times in our lives. John 16:33 says, "In this world you will have trouble." Acts 27, tells a story about the apostle Paul becoming shipwrecked. I often reflect on what Paul said when I am going through a tough time (and I paraphrase): "Take courage. Believe in God. But we will be shipwrecked!" Does your life ever feel like a shipwreck? Let me tell you a little about my personal shipwreck.

When Dare and I had our first child Linley, a beautiful little girl, we were so excited and elated. Soon after we took Linley home from the hospital, Dare and I began to notice Linley's stomach seemed to bother her. Dare mentioned this to her mom, and her mom explained to Dare that Dare had experienced an intolerance to lactose when she was an infant. Dare eventually grew out of it, and it is no longer an issue. Her mom said Linley may be suffering from the same thing. Her mother recommended we try switching Linley to a soy-based formula to see if Linley would improve. After we switched Linley to a soy-based formula, she was happy, feeding well, and sleeping soundly. Dare's mom saved the day!

When we took Linley in for her two-month checkup, we explained this to Linley's pediatrician, and he said it sounded like she was intolerant to lactose, but to be sure, he wanted us to have some tests run at the medical center in Houston where we were living at the time. He told us the tests were not complicated and could be completed quickly and easily so we could assure ourselves Linley was simply intolerant to lactose.

While Dare and her mom waited in the waiting room for Linley's tests to be completed, a priest appeared and told Dare how sorry he was to hear that Linley ceased breathing and asked Dare if he could pray for Linley! Dare was in shock! What happened to Linley during the simple test?

We later learned that the doctor assigned to Linley in the medical center had never done the test on such a young infant (Linley was three months old at the time). He used the wrong instrument, using an instrument for an adult rather than the instrument designed for an infant. As a result, a bunch of air was blown into Linley's stomach, causing her to throw up and aspirate. The code team at the hospital had been called, and after many attempts with the defibrillator and resuscitation techniques, they were able to revive Linley and relocate her into the pediatric intensive care unit (PICU).

As soon as Dare called me at work to tell me what happened, I rushed in a panic to the hospital. Words can't describe how we both felt, as we looked at our precious little girl inside the PICU, clinging to her life, connected to all those machines pumping drugs and fluids into her, and the respiratory intubation tube placed down her throat to provide mechanical ventilation to help her breathe. We were absolutely devastated, and we felt like a ton of concrete was pressing down on our hearts.

The PICU then was much different from PICUs today. The PICU consisted of one big room with pediatric infants lined up all along the walls. Dare and I could go inside to be with Linley and hold her little hand only certain hours each day. Many tears were shed. We were in constant prayer and a state of shock and disbelief that this happened to our precious Linley.

Dare and I slept on the floor in the waiting room of the PICU each night. Almost every day one of the pediatric patients would die, and the PICU staff would rush the family visitors of all the other pediatric patients out of the unit. Dare and I would go back out into the waiting room to sit and wait until the staff was able to cart the deceased infant out of the PICU. Seeing the child's body carted out and hearing the wailing of the deceased's family only added to the knots in our stomachs and the deep pain in our hearts. Eventually (usually hours later) the PICU would be reopened for us to go back inside to be with Linley for the remainder of her visiting hours. Dare and I continually asked ourselves, "Will Linley be next?" The doctors didn't have any positive news about Linley and could only advise that she was extremely critical. We continued to wait—hour by hour, day to day, week to week.

Then our day did indeed come—Linley had been in the PICU for about four months, and the doctors called us into a small conference room to advise us Linley was not going to make it. They advised us to take Linley home so she could pass away peacefully at home. As we took Linley home and began to make funeral arrangements for her, we were absolutely shipwrecked. Our precious, beautiful little Linley was not going to make it. I cannot even express the sense of loss and despair we felt.

Why God?

While I didn't lose my faith through this tragic event, I can tell you I became angry with God. I didn't understand why God would let this happen to us. I kept asking God, "How could You allow this to happen? Look at all the good things I do out of obedience—I go to church every Sunday, I read my Bible, I lead Bible studies, I pray every day. This is not fair! You have the wrong guy! I don't deserve this! Why, God?" I had the faith to believe that God was able to cure our daughter and save her and us from further suffering, and I prayed along those lines throughout every day. But I felt shipwrecked, and it took me a while to grow in my faith and to understand that God had a different plan for my daughter. It is certainly different from the plan I had for my Linley, and God wanted me to trust Him.

My anger at God began to evolve into guilt. I started wondering if I had done something to anger God, or if this was some punishment for my many sins I committed through the course of my life. Then one day while I was reading my Bible during my morning devotional and praying for a miracle cure for Linley, I came across John 9:1–3 in the Bible, where the disciples are walking with Jesus. They came across a man who was blind from birth, and the disciples asked Jesus, "Who sinned, this man or his parents, that he was born blind?"

This was exactly the question I had about Linley! This was something I was struggling with myself. I had been praying to God: "What have I done to deserve this tragedy in my life? What have I done to cause my precious Linley to be brought into this life and immediately have to suffer so much trauma and pain?"

And there was the answer in John 9:3—Jesus answered, "Neither this man nor his parents sinned, . . . but this happened so that the works of God might be displayed in him." There was my answer! It wasn't anything I did. God had a different plan for Linley, a plan where He wanted to utilize Linley in some way as part of His plan to bring Him glory.

New Management

That Scripture brought tremendous peace to me and eventually led to a tremendous change in me. You see, I am one of those driven, Type A people. I was one who always had a plan. I had a plan for my life, a plan for my family, and a plan for my career. God has blessed me with some incredible "git 'r done" gifts. But before Linley's tragedy, while I thought I was focused on God, deep down I was really focused on me and my own success. I was focused on what I needed to do to have a successful career and provide for my family. I was focused on how I could get ahead and get promoted up the leadership chain. Deep down I was really selfish and thinking more about myself than others. Empathy for others was not a tool I could have found in my toolbox, and it was certainly not a tool I thought I needed to use.

I thought I was a leader, and I was in control. You know the feeling—"I got this!" But Linley's tragedy showed me I didn't get it. I was not the one in control, and it wasn't about me as the leader. It was about others. It wasn't about my plan; it was about God's plan. It was about putting my trust in God *for everything.* I saw Jesus, who was God and all-powerful, yet He chose to serve others. That got my attention. I was the ultimate in *management waste,* thinking *I got this.* I saw I was not the one in control. My daughter participated as part of God's plan to show me I needed to submit to new management and authority—God.

It took Linley's medical tragedy to get my attention, to realize I was hardheaded, and I was not listening to God and trusting God. God took Linley's tragic medical event and turned it into a positive thing to work good in me and many others. I thought I was in control, and I had a plan. Sometimes it takes a catastrophic event to get us to correct course, and Linley's tragedy showed me I not only needed to correct course; I also needed new management. I needed to trust God rather than myself.

While Linley had a miraculous recovery from this event, she has had a lifetime of challenges with her brain injury and physical disabilities from all the drugs they used to revive her. It is still not easy for me to write about and relive this personal tragedy that totally changed me, and I hope by sharing my personal story, you can see how God can take our most severe tragedies and turn them into positive and life-changing events, if we will let Him.

I hope you won't need a catastrophe for God to get your attention, to see how much God loves you, wants a relationship with you, and wants you to trust Him rather than yourself. I hope this book and some of the experiences I will share in this book may even cause you to examine your own relationship with God and provide you with some ideas on how you can continue to grow in your own relationship with Him.

God took the tragedy with Linley and used it in a positive way to open my eyes about the type of leader God wanted me to be. I learned that the Bible has a lot to say about leadership. Jesus lived His life on earth modeling leadership for us. As Christians, we believe Jesus is the Son of God. We believe Jesus came to this earth and lived a perfect life, being fully God and fully human. Jesus is God, so He is fully sovereign. He is King. He is Lord. He is all-powerful. But even as King and Lord, and with all His power, Jesus lived His life on earth serving others. That is certainly not what you expect from an all-powerful King!

God's Design for Leadership

Jesus talked many times about how to be a leader. He not only talked about how to be a leader, but He lived His life here on earth exactly in accordance with what He taught us about leadership. We can read in the Bible about how Jesus lived His life and modeled servant leadership.

God gave us what is written in the Bible—it is His Word. If you buy a new car or appliance, the best place to learn about how it works in the way the engineers intended is to read the operator's manual. And yet most people do not take the time to read the operating manual God gave to us to learn about how He designed us to operate. God tells us, "All Scripture is God-breathed and is useful for teaching, rebuking, correcting and training in righteousness" (2 Timothy 3:16). The Bible is a great place to look to learn about God's intended design for leadership.

God made us and designed us in His image (Genesis 1:26), and He has provided the Bible to instruct us how

He wants us to live our lives—not just our lives at home or when we attend church, but how we are to live our lives every minute of every day, which includes how we are to live while we are at work.

The servant leadership model is the model of leadership Jesus taught and exemplified. Jesus is the Son of God. He came to this earth and lived a perfect life, being fully God and fully human. Jesus is God, so He is fully sovereign. Jesus is King, and Jesus is Lord. He is all-powerful. But even as King and Lord, Jesus modeled servant leadership. Jesus was humble, put others' needs first, and served others with humility.

In Matthew 20:25–28, Jesus described the difference between the typical leadership model we see today and servant leadership. James and John, two of the disciples who are brothers and the sons of Zebedee (see Mark 10:35), get their mother to ask Jesus if they could sit on His right and on His left when Jesus ascends to His throne in the kingdom. Jesus knows immediately that James and John are asking the question, not their mother, and Jesus responds directly to James and John, not to their mother.

James and John were asking (through their mother) for Jesus to place them into a position of power and authority with Jesus in His kingdom, and their arrogance infuriated the other ten disciples. Their question led Jesus to teach them about how He expects leaders to conduct themselves (in the same manner Jesus lived His life here on earth as a leader): "Jesus called them [His disciples] together and said, 'You know that the rulers of the Gentiles lord it over them [the people under the ruler's authority], and their high officials exercise authority over them'" (Matthew 20:25).

Jesus is saying the Gentiles have great men as their leaders who exercise their power and authority over the people they lead. But now let's look at how Jesus contrasts the Gentile model (and the typical leadership model we see today) with how God designed leadership and the proper organizational structure: "Not so with you. Instead, whoever wants to become great among you must be your servant, and whoever wants to be first must be your slave—just as the Son of Man did not come to be served, but to serve, and to give his life as a ransom for many" (Matthew 20:26–28).

Jesus, who is God, is telling us how to be a leader. He says that whoever wishes to become a great leader must be a servant! In fact, Jesus takes it even further than just being a servant—He says if you really want to be a great leader, you must be a slave! And to emphasize the point, Jesus says that He, as God and King, came to serve, not to be served. So this is where Jesus is saying the leadership model God wants us to use, and the model Jesus used, is the servant leadership model.

As I began to study God's instructions in the Bible about leadership, I began to see my own thinking about leadership evolve, beginning at my time at Baker Hughes, and continuing on throughout the remainder of my business career. I worked at Baker Hughes for almost ten years and then was recruited to Waste Management. We were able to put together an incredible team at Waste Management, and we were able to set the company on a new course for success. I am grateful to the former chairman of the board of Waste Management for hiring me and having the confidence in me to recommend to the board of directors to appoint me as the president of Waste Management.

While I was at Waste Management, I was in the premier episode of the *Undercover Boss* television series that appeared after the Super Bowl in 2010. I will tell you more about my experience on *Undercover Boss* and share some stories about my time at Waste Management later in this book. If you look at my career, I am ready for a change about every ten years, so I spoke to the board of directors to plan an orderly transition, and I left Waste Management after about ten and a half years, ready to pursue a new opportunity. I am delighted to see Waste Management has continued to thrive and perform exceedingly well after my departure.

After I left Waste Management, I went back to the oilfield to start a new oilfield services company from the ground up, which was a fun experience. It is now part of a public company called Select Energy Services. I retired as CEO when my daughter had another life-threatening event in 2015. She developed a hole in her heart, got down to about seventy-five pounds, and my wife and I were pretty sure this was going to be the end of her life here on this earth.

When she had another miraculous recovery, through many answered prayers, I felt God calling me to attend Dallas Theological Seminary. I graduated from Dallas Theological Seminary after three and a half years of intense study, and the experience has been a tremendous blessing in my life. I now spend about 10 percent of my time in business and the remainder in ministry.

So I provide this as a lot of background, not for the purpose of calling attention to myself but to provide a picture of some of what I have been through in my career and in my life. I want you to see that what I will share with you in this book is both biblically based and has some basis in reality. The principles in this book are not just theory; they are what God has given to us, and they have been successfully used in both large public companies and in a small entrepreneurial company that grew into a public company. None of the success, by the way, is based on my own effort alone, but rather as a result of allowing God to work in and through us, and being intentional about trusting God and serving others.

I have written this book to help Christian leaders see how God wants us to be servant leaders. I will be the first to tell you I have not been the type of servant leader God wanted me to be throughout my career, and I am not representing that I have all this figured out and I am the model of servant leadership for you to follow! I have failed to live up to the model of servant leadership many times throughout my career. Many times during my career I fell into the trap of wanting to *be somebody* rather than to *be a servant*. My purpose in writing this book is to set forth what I have learned throughout my career, through many of my own failings as a leader as well as the experiences I gained from working for some great leaders and also from working for some bad leaders.

If you spend enough time with anyone, you will see them at their best and at their worst. You will see some bright spots you want to emulate, and you will see some rough spots that will impact you in such a way you will never want to appear the same way to others. I can reflect back on many times in my life and realize I did not act in the way I should have, and I fell short of being the servant leader I discuss in this book. For those of you who were with me during those times, I sincerely apologize and ask for your forgiveness.

I have written this book to try to help others avoid some of the pitfalls I fell into during my career as I was trying to become the servant leader I knew God wanted me to be. This is the book I wish someone had given me early in my career so I could have avoided many of the mistakes I made as a leader. I am thankful the teams I worked with throughout my career were so forgiving of my shortcomings and my flaws. Hopefully, this book will help other leaders avoid the mistakes I made!

I will also explore what the Bible says about bosses—from bad bosses to good bosses, and even the Undercover Boss (yes, stay with me—I will show you where the Bible talks about the Undercover Boss!) And along the way I will share with you some of my personal experiences I hope will resonate with you as you look to become the servant leader God intends for your life.

My aim is to help you see how you can live your life in accordance with what the Bible teaches. As a Christian with God living inside you, you can give God a voice and turn control over to Him at work, rather than living life at work as if you left Him at home or in the car.

Our culture has now gotten to the point where if you are a Christian, you are expected to check your faith at the door, or leave it at home, or at least leave it in your car before you enter the workplace. Our culture has digressed from the concept of the separation of church and state (which by the way, was originally intended to protect the church from being oppressed by the government—it is amazing how far our culture has devolved from that concept), to now having a clear expectation for a separation of faith and work. Our present-day culture views it rude, insensitive, intrusive, not "politically correct," and perhaps even illegal to bring your faith into the workplace or to mention it all. I want to explore this with you in further chapters.

I hope you will apply some of what you read in the pages that follow to your own life. Then your own leadership style can be transformed so you can become the leader God designed you to be and avoid the pitfalls of *management waste*. I hope you will not only see how to be the servant leader God wants you to be in the work setting, but you will also see how these principles can apply to *all* relationships: spouse, family, friends, and colleagues.

"Now that I, your Lord and Teacher,
have washed your feet, you also should wash
one another's feet. I have set you an example
that you should do as I have done for you. . . .
Now that you know these things,
you will be blessed if you do them."

JOHN 13:14–15, 17

CHAPTER 2

Convertible Leadership

Top-Down Vs. Bottom-Up: God's Design for Leadership

THE TYPICAL model most people envision when they think of leadership is what I call "convertible leadership," or the top-down leadership model. The top-down leadership model focuses on the leader first, with the leader having power over others. In this model of leadership, the leader is viewed as having ascended to the top of the pyramid into a position of authority over others. Everyone serves the leader, and the leader directs others to perform in a way that serves the interests of the leader to bring the leader success and further elevate the leader.

In the top-down leadership model, if others are not serving the leader, then the leader really has no use for them. The leader is viewed as the boss, and the boss has power, privileges, and perks by being at the top of the pyramid.

At the opposite end of the leadership spectrum is the model of servant leadership. Servant leadership is bottom-up leadership (as opposed to the typical top-down leadership model). In the servant leadership model, the leader places the needs of others first and helps people develop and perform at their highest potential.

The difference between top-down leadership and bottom-up leadership can be thought of as the difference between pushing and pulling. In the top-down leadership model, the leader is in control and trying to push the members of the team to where the leader wants them to go, sometimes even using fear and intimidation to push them places they may not want to go. In the bottom-up leadership model, the leader is reaching out to pull the team members to an ever-higher level by modeling servant leadership and, by encouragement and empowerment, helping each team member excel to new heights and contribute their individual skills to the success of the team.

We previously saw in the discussion on Matthew 20:25–28 in chapter 1 how Jesus described the difference between top-down leadership and servant leadership. Jesus told the disciples the Gentiles have great men as their leaders who exercise their power and authority over the people they lead. Jesus was talking about the typical top-down leadership model we see used most of the time today. You may use the top-down leadership model today, or you may be in an organization that uses the top-down model.

Jesus contrasted top-down leadership with how God designed leadership and the proper organizational structure. He said that whoever wishes to become great must be a servant! Wow, notice how different the servant model is from typical top-down leadership! Jesus is saying that to be a great leader you must be a servant. Jesus even goes further to say that He, as God and King, came to serve, not to be served. I think Jesus is telling us the leadership model God wants us to use, and the model Jesus used, is the servant leadership model.

We see Jesus telling us in these verses that He does not want us to be top-down leaders, lording over and exercising authority over others. Instead, Jesus tells us to be servants and to serve others as leaders. This leadership model is a total game changer. People want to follow a servant leader not because they have to or because they fear the leader's title or power. They want to follow a servant leader because they trust the leader and know the leader cares about them.

No matter what your current position is (and even if you don't currently have a job outside the home or are currently retired, or in your current job you don't have anyone reporting to you), God has called each of us to live as a servant leader. God wants us to be servant leaders no matter what our position is.

In John 13:12–15, Jesus demonstrated how to serve others as the leader. To set the context for this passage, Jesus is again with the disciples (His team, if you will), and they just finished supper together. Jesus got up and washed each of the disciples' feet: "When he had finished washing their feet, he put on his clothes and returned to his place. 'Do you understand what I have done for you?' he asked them. 'You call me "Teacher" and "Lord," and rightly so, for that is what I am. Now that I, your Lord and Teacher, have washed your feet, you also should wash one another's feet. I have set you an example that you should do as I have done for you'" (John 13:12–15).

Jesus is telling us to be servant leaders. Many want to exercise power and authority, even some of the disciples, as we saw in the discussion in chapter 1 on Matthew 20:25–26. But not many leaders want to serve those on their team by taking a towel and a bowl of water and washing their feet. Jesus, who is God, took the time to care for His disciples and washed their feet. Is Jesus saying you need to wash the feet of those who you work with? No! The point is, we are to humble ourselves and show our colleagues how much we care about them. Jesus gave us the example, but are we following His example? How often are you using your servant's towel to help the people you work with?

Ever since I learned about empathy through the shipwreck with my daughter, my aim has been to use the servant leadership model when in a position of leadership. God used the terrible medical accident and tragedy with Linley to teach me it wasn't about me; it was about others. Caring for others is at the top of my list now and is what really brings me joy. I wouldn't have found empathy without going through this continuing trial with Linley. I am not telling you I have it all figured out now, and I am not telling you I still don't struggle with pain at times as I think about Linley.

Yes, I still experience times of pain and suffering that Linley, my wife, my son, and I all endure. Linley's life has not been the plan I imagined for her. She has been in intensive care with life-threatening issues on average about every three to four years of her life. Seeing her suffer is always tough. At other times I feel my own pain when I see the daughters of my siblings and friends go through high school as athletes, cheerleaders, or whatever else they chose to pursue, go on to college, start their careers, marry, and now they are having grandkids. Sometimes I think, *What if . . .* , but then

I remember I am just being selfish. This isn't about me and my plan; this is about God and God's plan and trusting God rather than relying on myself.

I am not going to tell you I have all the answers about why Linley's life turned out the way it has or why God allowed this to happen to Linley. But I can tell you I have no doubt in my mind that God's plan included my daughter participating with Him as He worked in and through her in a way that has not only drawn me into a much closer relationship with God but has also made a huge positive impact on many other people.

Linley is the most happy and positive person you would ever want to meet. Even with all her physical and mental disabilities, surgeries, stays in intensive care, and all her pain and suffering, you never hear her complain about pain. She is my inspiration! I can definitely see God's work displayed in her life! When I take her to the grocery store, everybody in the store knows her. When I look at my son, he is one of the most empathetic and caring men I have ever known, most likely from Linley's impact on his life (my son has also taught me a lot about empathy).

I have seen the power of people who are fully engaged team members because they know those in leadership care about them, so they in turn want the leader to know they can be counted on to deliver their top performance. Now I realize certain types of people are willing to put up with having a boss "lord over them" because they believe, if they just endure and persevere, they will eventually get their time at the top of the pyramid so they can "lord it over" others.

Top-down leaders who are insecure tend to rule by fear, intimidation, and lashing out, trying to show they are in control, believing people fear punishment. Through such fear-and-intimidation tactics, they believe, the team will work harder and be driven to success.

This is the opposite of being a servant leader. A servant leader will help position each member of the team for success, encouraging and empowering all team members to be the best they can be, which will further build the trust among the team members and drive the success of the entire team.

Servant leaders are secure in their relationship with God, and they are secure enough in themselves to know they need to surround themselves with people who are smarter than they are and who have different skills than they do so the team can win together. Insecure leaders tend to surround themselves with people just like themselves. They will tend to micromanage the team members to control the team so the leader can point to himself or herself as being the cause for the success, when that will most likely conclude in failure.

Bad Bosses

Even if you currently have a boss who follows the top-down leadership model, don't give up hope. I had several bosses during my career who exercised top-down leadership, and I probably learned more from them than the best bosses I worked with. I learned how I did *not* want to lead once I was given the opportunity. So don't give up hope! Everyone works with bad bosses at some point in their careers. Never forget how they made you feel, as if they didn't care about you. Never forget how that leadership approach impacted the way you performed and your attitude. Some of the best lessons I learned about leadership came from working under some horrible leaders.

I had a boss one time who ruled by fear and intimidation. He would regularly belittle someone in meetings, just to make clear to everyone he was the boss. He rarely told people how much he appreciated them, and he was hard to get to know on a personal level. As a result, people were afraid to ever question him or volunteer their ideas. I saw how his leadership style negatively impacted people on the team, and I knew I did not ever want to make people on my team feel that way.

Great Bosses

I had another boss who worked hard at trying to get know people on a personal level. He wanted to know about our family and our career aspirations so he could help us fill our gaps so we could progress in our own careers. In meetings he always encouraged people to voice their ideas and concerns so we could brainstorm and arrive at the best solutions. He never took all the credit for our success and recognized each of us for our contributions.

He was collaborative and encouraging to all of us, and he always was transparent by explaining where we were headed, what he expected from each of us, so we knew how to contribute to the success of the team. He served as a great coach and teacher to bring each of us along in our careers. We always knew if we made a mistake, he had our back. Every member on the team gave 110 percent, and we all cared about one another. It was a great place to work. We all worked hard, and we had a lot of fun winning together.

So, what does it mean to be a servant leader? The servant leader serves others first and doesn't expect to be served by them. Leadership is about caring for others and focusing primarily on the growth and well-being of the people on their team. The servant leader shares power, puts the needs of others first, and helps people develop and perform at their highest potential. This is what Jesus taught and how Jesus lived. I want you to see that the leader-first model and the servant-first model are at the opposite ends of the leadership style spectrum.

So, how are these leadership styles evidenced in business or any team setting (even on sports teams)? As Jesus said, the servant leader's highest priority is to serve other people's needs, not to be served by them. The best test I have used is to ask myself, "Am I helping the people on my team grow as persons? Am I helping them grow in their career? Am I helping them grow in their faith? Am I helping them see Jesus at work? By modeling the servant behavior as their leader, am I helping them learn how to become servant leaders, and ultimately, see Jesus and the Holy Spirit operating in my life? How would others describe my leadership style?"

I have found servant leadership to be a total game changer. I have seen this leadership style develop the highest performing teams I have ever been on because people cared about one another and wanted to win together. Would you rather work for a boss who wants to use you for his or her own purposes or a boss who cares about you and your development?

We each get to decide what type of leader we are going to be. How do you want people to remember you as a leader?

What do you fear in choosing to be a servant leader? Do you fear losing power? By sharing the power, you will gain the respect of the members on your team. Do you fear not being given the credit for the team's successes? By being a servant leader, you can allow God to turn your trash (what others thought of you as a top-down leader who doesn't care about anyone but yourself) into treasure (an inspiring leader who cares about others and leads the team to tremendous success together).

By leading the way Jesus led, and the way God wants us to lead, we can allow God to work through us in our actions and words to make a difference in other people's lives. The fundamental question we must continually ask, is: "Who is managing your life, you or God?" To become great leaders, we must turn our lives over to God as servant leaders and serve others.

So now I want to peel the onion back a bit further by delving into five of the characteristics I think evidence the type of servant leadership I believe Jesus is talking about. Much has been written in other books about other characteristics of servant leadership in addition to these, but these five characteristics of servant leadership resonate with me. They are the characteristics I have tried to develop and use through my own leadership. The acronym I use to help me remember them is CLEAN: *Commitment, Listening, Empathy, Accountability*, and *Notice*. The acronym CLEAN ties servant leadership together for me, helping me remember to use the CLEAN principles to clean up my act and eliminate *management waste*. We will examine each of these five characteristics in depth in the next five chapters.

Commitment
Listening
Empathy
Accountability
Notice

CHAPTER 3

Wasted Management

Commitment

THE FIRST characteristic of servant leadership is *commitment*. *Commitment* means being focused on helping others grow as people, not just in business skills but also in their faith. Failing to help others grow is a waste of the leadership position God has placed you in.

The apostle Paul tells us, "Be devoted to one another in love. Honor one another above yourselves" (Romans 12:10). Paul also tells us to "carry each other's burdens, and in this way you will fulfill the law of Christ" (the law of Christ is to love God and to love one another) (Galatians 6:2).

One of the ways I believe my team knew I was committed to them is I kept a legal pad where I wrote down various people's names and information about the people I met and wanted to keep track of in the company. The list contained hundreds and hundreds of names of people I met and interacted with in my trips to field operations. The names ranged from frontline people and support people in the field and the corporate office to upper management throughout the company. My list included people who reported to me, as well as people who didn't report to me, and included people in operations, sales, customer service, accounting, human resources, information technology, and other areas throughout the company.

When I was at Waste Management, my travel averaged more than two hundred days a year, meeting with our operations personnel and our customers. Each time I visited one of our offices, I made a point to go around and speak to employees individually—at their desks, in the break rooms, in our customer call centers, mechanics working on the trucks and heavy equipment, sorters working on the recycling lines, truck and heavy equipment operators before they went out on their routes or out to the landfill to operate their equipment. Wherever the employees were, I sought them out to speak with them directly. And when I came across employees who were engaged and seemed to be ready to move up in their areas of responsibility, I made a note of that on my legal pad.

I would then seek out the supervisors of those on my list and ask them to tell me how Joe or Mary was progressing in their careers. I asked what we were doing to help them grow and develop so they could move up to the next position. And when I returned to that location, I would follow up again with the supervisor to see what progress had been made to move them up in their career since my last visit.

I knew I couldn't keep up with all fifty thousand plus employees, but I tried to model the behavior of commitment to others so other leaders in the company would do the same thing. This is exactly what Jesus did, as He modeled the behavior of servant leadership: "When he [Jesus] had finished washing their feet, he put on his clothes and returned to his place. 'Do you understand what I have done for you?' he asked them. 'You call me "Teacher" and "Lord," and rightly so, for that is what I am. Now that I, your Lord and Teacher, have washed your feet, you also should wash one another's feet. I have set you *an example* that you should do as I have done for you'" (John 13:12–15; emphasis added).

So, I ask you, "Are you modeling the behavior you want to see from your team?" By showing commitment to your team, you will develop a sense of trust within your team. I found by following up with people, and continuing the dialogue I had with them the last time I met with them, some people would ask me to tell them more about my faith. God gave me many opportunities to allow Him to work through me to help others in their faith because there was trust between us, and they felt comfortable asking me to tell them more about my faith. By being committed to others, they saw this was not all about me. It was about helping them grow and position them for success.

Developing Leaders and Disciples

One thing we did at Waste Management was create what we called the Leadership Forum. Each year, we selected ten to fifteen people we thought could become future leaders in the company. We put them through a twelve-month training program on leadership and business and assigned them a business mentor from within our company to coach them in their current positions. This was almost like a program of disciples making disciples but geared toward leadership. The top leaders in the company spent time with each of these future leaders during the twelve-month program to help them develop as leaders.

This was a highly successful program, as the people who were selected felt valued by the company and learned a lot from some of the great leaders in the company. In fact, one of the people who went through this program eventually became the CEO of Waste Management after I left the company. I will tell you more about him later in this chapter.

Whenever I discussed career aspirations with employees, I asked them what gaps needed to be filled to position them for progress toward their career goals. I also tried to assess their level of commitment to their own goals and their personal commitment to fill those gaps. It is one thing to have goals and aspirations, but if you aren't committed to do what is necessary to fill the gaps to achieve your goals, you will never be successful. To progress in your career, you have to be willing to make the commitment.

Start Small

Another aspect of servant leadership commitment is being committed to even the little things. Before someone (and even God) will place you in authority over bigger things, you must demonstrate you can do a great job on the little things.

Jesus tells a parable about a man who was about to go on a journey, so he entrusted his money to some of his servants to watch over his money while he was away. When the man returned from his journey, he met with each of his servants to see how they did with the man's money, and for those who invested his money wisely, the master told them, "Well done, good and faithful servant! You have been faithful with a few things; I will put you in charge of many things. Come and share your master's happiness!" But one servant did nothing with the money his master entrusted to him. The master said to him, "You wicked, lazy servant. . . . You should have put my money on deposit with the bankers, so that when I returned I would have received it back with interest. So take the bag of gold from him and give it to the one who has ten bags" (Matthew 25:14–28).

This parable illustrates that we are to be committed to doing our best with whatever God has given to us—whatever our position in our company, our financial resources, etc. Then, when we demonstrate we are capable with the smaller things, we will be given larger areas of responsibility. I have found the most effective leaders have been followers first. By that I mean they demonstrated commitment and success with the little things first rather than just being focused on how to get to the bigger things (areas of increased responsibility).

I can't tell you how many young people I have interviewed for a starting position in the company who tell me they want to work a year or two and then have their own company. I have seen many others who spend more of their time asking how they can get promoted to a vice president position rather than focusing on doing a great job in their existing position and letting their performance show how capable they are.

The people I have seen move up in their careers the fastest are those who are committed to doing the best job they can in their current position, seek out advice from others as to how they could improve their performance in their existing job, and are coachable (they listen to the advice and implement it), and have such a positive can-do attitude that everyone wants them on their team. They are not only committed to do the best in whatever job they are in; they are committed to the team and everyone around them, always being willing to pitch in to help others, and not constantly self-promoting themselves.

One of the best examples I have seen of this type of commitment is a young person we hired as a financial analyst at Waste Management not long after I arrived. The company was a mess, as I previously discussed, and we needed lots of help in the financial analysis area. He quickly demonstrated his great talent in the area of financial analysis, and he helped us immensely. He showed he was bright and dedicated and willing to work hard to get us the information we needed out of our limited information systems, which were a total mess when we first arrived.

A few years after joining us, he came to me and asked me if I would ever consider him for a position in operations. I explained to him how different operations management was from the financial analysis work he performed and that it would require him to develop new leadership skills outside his comfort zone. I asked him if he would be willing to move into a small operation in the northeast. We could start with something small where he would have a great chance to learn about operations, develop his leadership skills, and demonstrate success. He and his supportive wife were willing to move their family for the opportunity to learn new skills. He was committed to filling his gaps.

He was teachable and coachable. He was willing to go through our system of development. And his spouse and family were supportive of the process, as we moved him up through the organization into increasing areas of responsibility following his showing of successes and building trust with his team at each stage of his development. Some of the places he and his family moved were maybe not the first place you would choose, but his family supported him, and he saw the benefit of what he would learn by taking on the new position of increased responsibility. Eventually, we even chose him to be part of our twelve-month Leadership Form, discussed earlier in this chapter. He is a tremendous success story, in that he eventually became CFO of Waste Management. And with his proven operations successes, financial acumen, and leadership skills, he went on to become the CEO of Waste Management (and continues to hold that position today).

His career success can be attributed to his own commitment to:

1. Fill the gaps in his experience.
2. Seek out advice on how to improve and then take action to implement the advice given—being coachable.
3. Stay focused on the job at hand and strive to be the best he could be and learn everything he could in each successive role of increasing responsibility rather than continually ask about the next job.

4. Commit to each member of his team and the success of the team—building trust and promoting his team rather than himself.
5. Become the best and respected leader he could possibly become by being committed to serving others.

Jesus, even though He is God, was a servant to others while He lived on this earth. He modeled how we are to serve as servant leaders. Jesus' plan was to live a perfect life on this earth for thirty years, pick twelve people to teach and train for three years, spend the next three days dealing with our sin, and then ascend back to heaven and turn things over to the twelve disciples to teach others, and for the others to teach the world. We can't impact everyone as leaders, but if we model servant leadership to those we come in contact with, then they can model servant leadership to others, and so on. In this way you will build an incredible company of servant leaders.

Modeling the characteristics of servant leadership discussed in this book is something I have endeavored to do with my team. Just as I tried to show commitment to people's careers, I also tried to coach them along the way to help train them and position them for roles of increased responsibility. Seeing members of our team get promoted and continue to achieve success has always given me great joy. In fact, I am still in contact with many people I worked with over the last almost four decades who still call me to bounce things off of me, or seek guidance from me, and I am always honored they would call and ask.

Step Outside the Comfort Zone

Another aspect of being committed to the career development of others of vital importance in helping them grow is to provide future leaders with a wide range of experiences outside their comfort zone. I think leaders grow when they are moved into different roles within the company for a period of time that are totally different from what they have previously experienced.

I can provide many examples of where I have seen this work well, including the example of the person who went on to become the CEO of Waste Management from starting out as a young financial analyst. These people were willing to get out of their comfort zone to learn new skills and were coachable.

An example showing how well this approach can work comes from my time at Rockwater. When we first started Rockwater, I was the first employee. While I was the CEO, I was also wearing all the other hats in the beginning. That is what you have to do as an entrepreneur, but I can also tell you I was not doing it all very well. I needed to build a team with people who possessed skills I didn't have. I also wanted to build a team with people I thought possessed the capability to continue to grow in their careers as we grew Rockwater into what we hoped would eventually become a public company.

The first person I hired was a seasoned CFO, having served as CFO for a public company before joining us at Rockwater. I was looking for a talented public-company CFO who could eventually succeed me as CEO of Rockwater after we got Rockwater up and running and when I was in a position to retire.

As part of the interview process, she told me she would eventually be interested in becoming a CEO. I told her I could help prepare her to be considered for my CEO position down the road, but she would need to be willing to move from her position as CFO at some point and spend some time in operations to learn how the business functions through our people serving our customers and to help her develop her leadership skills further.

When we grew Rockwater to the point that I thought we were ready to move her from her CFO position into operations, I explained to her I knew this was totally outside her comfort zone, but if she could earn the trust of the field operations and demonstrate success in an operations role in addition to the success she demonstrated as CFO, she would be a strong candidate for the board of directors of Rockwater to consider (along with others) to succeed me. I also explained to her that other companies would certainly be interested in her as well, with both her CFO and operations experience.

She was willing and committed to the challenge, and we moved her into a position to lead the entire chemical segment of our business. She understood this move was not without risks, since she was moving to a position in which she did not have experience, was outside her comfort zone, and she would no longer be the CFO. But I also encouraged her and told her I would be there to help mentor and coach her, and I wanted to see her succeed. I told her I would consider her failure as my failure.

She did a great job in her new role, further developed her leadership skills in the process, earned the respect and trust of the operations part of the business, and made it easy for the board of directors to select her as my successor when I retired as CEO of the company. She continues as the CEO of the public successor company today.

Let me take a bit of a sidebar here to say I have always appreciated the commitment my family has given to me throughout my career. My wife, Dare, has always been supportive of me and my career. She never complained about all my business travel, and she even encouraged me to accept new positions of responsibility that required me to move to California and Arizona to further my career. This was significant since our move put an additional burden on her as Linley's primary caregiver. Linley was dealing with significant health issues and was constantly in and out of the hospital in Houston. I couldn't have progressed in my career without Dare's steadfast commitment, support, and encouragement, and I give her tremendous credit for the successes we achieved together.

Let me just say, any person in leadership who is blessed with a supportive spouse, family, friend, boss, or colleague should thank God every day for that gift. I encourage you to thank your spouse, your family, and whoever has shown commitment to you and encouraged you thus far in your own career. We often don't thank them enough for their commitment and the sacrifices they have made to help support us along our journey.

Create a Safe Environment

When you commit to people, you must make it safe for them to make mistakes. People are going to make mistakes, particularly when you place them into a new role that may be outside their comfort zone. You can't have a return on investment without taking some risk.

As I will discuss in chapter 4 about listening, if you blow up when a mistake is made, anyone making a mistake will most likely shut down and then fail in the new position. Their failure will be a poor reflection on your commitment to coaching, mentoring, and developing others. You must support them, and you have to expect mistakes from time to time. The important thing is to make sure the members of your team know you expect mistakes and you have their back. They need to know you expect them to identify and correct mistakes quickly and bring those mistakes to your attention so you can communicate those mistakes to others where necessary to prevent making the same mistake again. Such communication should be done in a way that does not throw the person under the bus and should reinforce the commitment you have to them.

While I was at Waste Management, we did a detailed study on the impact of our customer relationship when we missed picking up their trash or recycling just one time. We found that having a strong recovery program for missed pickups solidified the customer relationship. If we recovered well, the customer stayed with us longer than if we never missed a pickup. When you make a mistake, admit it, ask for forgiveness, recover quickly, and you will build trust and loyalty.

Set Clear Expectations

I believe most people show up to work wanting to do a great job. They want to have a voice, be heard, and know how to contribute to the success of the team. Commitment to others means we need to explain our expectations to each member of our team and be clear on how they can contribute to the team's success and be successful themselves.

Often, when new members join an existing team, they are not told much about how the team interacts and works together, what the team is trying to achieve, and how they can specifically contribute to the success of the team. New team members quickly feel left out. They don't know how to contribute, they don't feel like they have a voice, and so they withdraw and shut down. New team members may have some critical skills and capabilities they could contribute to the team, but they have not been empowered (discussed below) and shown the way to contribute and discharge their duties. The leader and other team members have wasted a tremendous opportunity by not drawing the new person into the culture of the team so they can contribute their unique skills to the team's success. This is *management waste*!

How many times do we bring new members onto our team and don't take the time to explain to them how the team works together and interacts with one another and how they can contribute to the team's success? We simply expect them to know the rules or figure out the rules on their own (just as we had to do), and then we wonder why they withdraw or quit.

Those new team members may have had the highest potential or may have had something important to contribute, but they just shut down. And then we think they just aren't the type of people who will engage with the team. We think they are lazy or just want to breeze along and not contribute. We think something is wrong with them, when the truth is *we* failed them!

One of the first questions I always ask a leader, when I learn they have let someone go, is: "Did the terminated employee fail us, or did we fail them (by not articulating clearly what was expected, coaching them on how to contribute, listening to them, and giving them the tools and training so they could succeed)?" Was this a case of a lazy employee or *management waste*?

One of the techniques I have used throughout my career to help position members of my team for success is setting clear expectations and goals for each member of my team. It is critically important each person knows exactly what they need to do to contribute to the success of the team. If you don't set clear expectations for each member of your team, most likely they will be guessing at what they think your expectations are. You will probably end up being frustrated by their performance because they guessed wrong, or they simply couldn't read your mind. So you both end up failing—you failed with *management waste* by positioning them for failure rather than positioning them for success, and they failed because they couldn't achieve your unstated expectations!

I am amazed at how often that happens in our businesses and in our marriages and relationships today! Failure results because unstated expectations were not met! Making your expectations known is vital in all relationships in order to avoid frustration and failure.

A tool I like to use when setting business performance goals with people is called SMART goals. Many companies use this tool today, and you may already be familiar with it. SMART goals are:

- **Specific**: The goal describes specifically what the person needs to accomplish and describes it in a way that we will both clearly know whether the goal has been achieved.
- **Measurable**: The goal includes a metric to allow us both to track the progress toward achieving the goal and to determine whether the person is on track, ahead of schedule, or falling behind in their progress toward achieving the goal.
- **Achievable**: The goal must be something that can realistically be achieved, not something that is just aspirational.
- **Results focused**: The goal must be something that, when achieved, will contribute to the success of the overarching goals for the team.
- **Time bound**: The goal must include a specific time for the goal to be achieved and is even better if it includes milestone progress dates to help track progress along the way.

For example, when I moved my colleague out of her role as CFO and into her new role running our chemical business at Rockwater, as I discussed earlier in this chapter, I felt it was important for both of us to work together to develop goals for her new role, and I wanted those goals to be SMART goals.

In order to meet this objective, SMART goals must support and contribute to the achievement of the overarching goals of the team. This means we first had to discuss, and develop with input from other team members, the shared purpose and overarching goals of her new team. Her entire team had to have an understanding, provide input into the development of, and buy into why the team was in place and what the team was working toward. Each team member had to understand what would be considered a win for the team, what the team was trying to achieve, and then ultimately, each team member had to make a commitment to do their part to contribute to the success of the team by committing to their own SMART goals.

I always viewed developing SMART goals for our team and for each member of the team before the beginning of the year was like going to school and having the professor give each student the questions to the final exam on the first day of class and then teaching the students throughout the semester on how to get an A on the final exam at the end of the semester. I never understood why none of my professors took that approach in school. It just seems so simple—tell me what you want me to learn and how you will judge my performance. Then teach me what I need to know so I can succeed and meet your expectations! Who wouldn't want to have a teacher like that in school? And who wouldn't want to have a leader who made their expectations clear, gave you details on how you were going to be measured, and then helped you succeed?

While I believe reaching agreement on these goals before the beginning of the year is important, I also believe there should be discussions about progress and any unforeseen difficulties throughout the year. The goals shouldn't be put away in a file somewhere, only to be pulled out at the end of the year to see how you did. There should never be any surprises on either side at the end of the year.

This is the process I liked to use at both the midyear and end-of-year review. I would first ask the team member to provide me with a written self-evaluation of their performance and progress on each of their goals so they could outline their own view of their performance. The midyear review would also include a discussion of any obstacles that had arisen that had not been foreseen when we first agreed upon the goal so we could make any necessary adjustments to the goal at the midyear review. We would then sit down in person and discuss their self-evaluation, and I would provide my additional input and response to their self-evaluation.

At the end-of-year review, I also gave each individual an opportunity to provide me a written response to my written evaluation if they so desired (but not required). As part of the end-of-year review I would discuss the individual's career aspirations and any gaps either of us felt needed to be addressed to position them to be considered for the next step in their career.

Project Yellow Tail

Another important aspect of being committed to others is sharing the power with them. The apostle Paul tells us to "entrust . . . to faithful men who will be able to teach others also" (2 Timothy 2:2 NASB). We also see Jesus giving power and authority to his disciples: "When Jesus had called the Twelve together, he gave them power and authority to drive out all demons and to cure diseases" (Luke 9:1).

Let me share one of my favorite stories from my time at Waste Management that illustrates the power of empowering others. It is a story about a visit I made to one of our operations in Florida that serviced a large retirement community. The purpose of my visit (as was fairly typical of my field operation visits) was to conduct a performance review with the local leadership team, to meet with some of our largest customers in the area, to meet with our employees to discuss our progress, and to get our employees' input on ways to continue to improve our company.

As I typically did before I visited any of our operations, I reviewed the financial and operational metrics for this particular business unit before I arrived. One of the metrics I always looked at first when reviewing operational performance was the team's safety metric. I discovered from our data there was a direct correlation between having great safety performance and the quality of the leadership team. Whenever I saw great safety performance, it turned out the team's financial and operational performance were usually in the top quartile as well.

Looking at the team's safety performance first gave me a quick view of what to expect from this operation. It was an amazing discovery for me to see correlation of the safety metric to operational and financial performance. If an operation demonstrated a great safety record, I usually found an engaged team of employees who respected and were committed to one another and their leaders. They were a collaborative team that delivered excellent operational and financial performance. It also followed that if an operation reflected a poor safety record, employees were usually not as engaged, leaders were usually not well respected, and their operational and financial performance usually suffered as a result.

As I reviewed the safety performance of this particular operation before I arrived for our performance review meeting, I noticed that their safety record was terrible. As I dug further into the data to try to determine what was driving their poor safety performance, I noticed their safety statistics showed a high number of accidents where third-party vehicles were running into the back of our trucks, and this was happening frequently. We certainly experience this on occasion at other locations, but I had never seen this many occurrences so frequently.

When I arrived at the operation facility and sat down at the conference table with the leadership team, the first thing I asked them was why they thought so many third-party vehicles were running into the back of our trucks while they were out on their routes.

The local management team responded to my question by explaining to me that most of their routes were in and around a large retirement community, where most of the residents should probably have given up their driver's licenses years ago. They explained these were elderly people who did not have good vision and experienced difficulty in operating a vehicle. Even though each of our trucks was equipped with reflective tape with contrasting colors and flashing lights on the back, these elderly people were still running into the back of our trucks when they were stopped to pick up a trash container at the curb. They explained to me their operation was just a victim given the circumstances of the community where they operated, and there was nothing they could do about it.

I then told the management team I had heard that Albert Einstein once said doing the same thing over and over again and expecting a different result is insanity. I told them I was fairly certain if they just kept doing the same things they always did, we should not expect to see a different result. They agreed with my thoughtful analysis and said their safety results had looked like that for years.

I then closed up my notebook with the materials for the performance review and told them I was leaving. I asked them to come up with something new to try—anything they thought could possibly bring a different result. I told them I wasn't as concerned at this point with the result of what they might try, because I didn't think things could get much worse. So I encouraged them to brainstorm and come up with a list of things to try that might provide a better result, then pick what they thought was the best alternative and try it. I told them they were empowered to try anything that might have the potential of reducing these accidents, as it just might save someone's life. I told them I would return in four weeks to see what they came up with.

When I returned four weeks later, I noticed something as soon as I turned into the parking lot. I noticed that the rear part of five trucks had been painted yellow. When I walked into the conference room to meet with the local management team, I asked them to tell me what they had come up with and to share what they had learned.

They told me they painted the back of five trucks yellow (we were in the middle of a branding campaign, and we were painting all the trucks and containers green, just as you see today, but they added yellow to the back of these five trucks). I asked if they noticed any difference in their safety results. They said, "You are not going to believe this, but those are the only five trucks in our fleet that have not been run into from behind since you left us four weeks ago!" I said, "You have got to be kidding! Why did you only paint five trucks?"

They said they knew how important our new branding campaign was, and how we wanted all the trucks and containers throughout the company to be painted green so they all looked the same, and this yellow paint scheme was not part of the branding campaign. They wanted to see the results and then discuss the results with me before proceeding further, since I said I would be back in four weeks.

I told them to paint all their trucks that way, and let's see what happens. And you know what happened? The new paint scheme almost completely eliminated the problem of those trucks being hit from behind. Now I don't understand why painting the rear of the trucks yellow made that big of an impact because the trucks already were equipped with lots of reflective tape with contrasting colors on the back and lots of flashing lights. But the point is, this team was empowered to try something different, and that empowerment made a huge difference.

In fact, we ended up painting the entire Waste Management fleet (more than 25,000 trucks) the same way, in what we called Project Yellow Tail, and that significantly reduced crashes from the rear across our entire fleet. That paint scheme is still the design used on all Waste Management trucks today, and now they are ordered from the factory with the same paint design.

Other trucking fleets (competitors to Waste Management, and trucking fleets in different industries) have now copied that design (the highest form of flattery), which I think is great as I am sure it has saved many lives. So if you see a truck with a yellow tail (Waste Management or otherwise), you now know where it came from. It came from a group of leaders in Florida who were empowered to try something, anything, to get a different result.

We also recognized the team from Florida throughout the company for their great idea and for saving untold accidents and injuries. Employees around the company brought forward many other great ideas because people felt empowered to try new things and to take reasonable risks to achieve improved results. They recognized that their leaders were committed to them and had their backs, and it led to many other operational improvements and innovations as people felt empowered to try new things.

Jesus modeled empowerment with His disciples. Jesus' plan was to come to this earth and live a perfect life for thirty years, pick twelve disciples to teach and train for three years, spend the next three days dealing with our sin, and then ascend back to heaven, and turn things over to the disciples to continue with the mission of teaching others so the gospel could be spread throughout the world. The last message Jesus said to his disciples (and to us) before ascending to heaven was: "Therefore go and make disciples of all nations, baptizing them in the name of the Father and of the Son and of the Holy Spirit, and teaching them to obey everything I have commanded you. And surely I am with you always, to the very end of the age." (Matthew 28:19–20).

Jesus spent three years teaching and mentoring His disciples, and then He empowered them to carry on as He ascended into heaven. While I feel strongly that this verse commands all of us as Christians to go and make disciples, the point I want to make is that Jesus modeled how we are to pour ourselves into others and be committed to them and then empower them with authority to do the same.

Having commitment to others is the first step of being a servant to others. People know whether you are committed to them or just using them to promote yourself and your own career. When your team knows you are committed to them and care about them, you have the beginning of a trusting team that not only cares about one another because of the commitment you are modeling, but you have the making of a high-performing team. Commitment is the first step to the CLEAN process to eliminate *management waste*. In the next chapter we will take a look at the importance of listening and what it really means to listen.

Commitment
Listening
Empathy
Accountability
Notice

CHAPTER 4

Trash Talking

Listening

IN THIS chapter we will examine the second characteristic of servant leadership: **listening**. Many leaders, upon
achieving their leadership status, begin to think, *It's all about
me.* Their ego begins to take control of them and causes
them to believe they got to their leadership position because
they are the smartest one in the room. They begin to believe
nobody can tell them anything they don't already know—
they already have all the answers, and everyone else just
needs to listen to them and follow their leadership. They may
even belittle others to make themselves feel elevated above
everyone else.

At this point everyone on the team begins to see the
emperor is sick and not listening, and nobody wants to tell
the emperor he or she has lost their clothes (and maybe even
their mind) with how they are caught up in believing their
own trash talk. The dictionary defines *trash talk* as "insult-
ing or boastful speech intended to demoralize, intimidate, or

humiliate someone." The effect of this trash-talking leadership style is that it shuts everyone else down.

When a leader rules by intimidation and doesn't value input from others, everyone on the team is afraid to voice their ideas or concerns because of how it will be received by the boss. The entire team begins to just show up for work for a paycheck rather than being engaged and energized and wanting to give their best for the success of the team. No new ideas are offered up, and if there are problems that could have been corrected before things really got bad, they are not mentioned or are swept under the rug, sometimes leading to disaster and even failed companies.

On the other end of the spectrum is the servant leader, who focuses on listening to others. This doesn't mean just letting others talk and not interrupting. Jesus' half brother James, who is believed to have written the book of James in the Bible, tells us what it means to listen: "Everyone should be quick to listen, slow to speak and slow to become angry" (James 1:19). James is telling us we should listen to others to gain wisdom.

Many verses in the book of Proverbs teach us about listening to others to gain wisdom, including the following:

- "Let the wise listen and add to their learning, and let the discerning get guidance" (Proverbs 1:5). We are to obtain guidance from others.
- "The way of fools seems right to them, but the wise listen to advice" (Proverbs 12:15). We are to seek and listen to advice from others.

- "Listen to advice and accept instruction, that you may gain wisdom in the future" (Proverbs 19:20 ESV). Wisdom comes from listening to others.

I could go on and on, as there are many places in the Bible where God tells us we should listen more than we talk. I have heard it said perhaps the reason God gave us two ears, but only one mouth, is so we will listen twice as much as we speak!

One of the things I did throughout my business career is I spent a lot of time out with the frontline employees asking them what caused them the most frustration in their jobs, and if they were given the power to change just one thing to help our employees better serve our customers, what would it be?

I learned that from my dad. I started working in our family's construction business in the second grade, sweeping floors. I progressed to jobs that included framing carpenter, electrician, plumber, heavy equipment operator, and job foreman. Those various jobs my dad placed me in helped mold me as a person and a leader.

Everyone in the company knew I was the boss's son. I hated that. Being the boss's son was the last thing I wanted to be viewed as. I was determined to work harder than everyone else. I wanted people to want me on their team because of my work ethic, dedication, and willingness to do the jobs nobody else wanted to do (like volunteering to go up in an attic of a house in the middle of the summer when it felt like it was over 120 degrees up there, lying down in itchy insulation to fix a broken plumbing pipe.) Those jobs also taught me to appreciate the tough jobs the frontline folks do every day and how important their jobs are to the success of any company.

My dad always impressed upon me how important it is to let the frontline employees, who do the tough jobs and are many times the face to the customer, know how much they are appreciated. He also taught me to continually get input from them on ways to improve our products and services. He told me that a big part of my job was to help remove those things that cause them frustration in their daily work. That is solid advice I have used throughout my career.

The operating model we came up with to integrate all the various companies Waste Management acquired before I arrived to streamline our operations was based on the input we received by asking the right questions to our employees who were doing the tough frontline jobs. The new operating model brought about incredible improvements in productivity, safety, job satisfaction, and customer service and led to Waste Management becoming a top-performing public company.

It was not because I had all the answers. In fact, I knew very little about the Waste Management business when I first arrived, other than I knew if I put my trash cans out on the street at the right times, my trash would disappear. Who better to ask how to improve your company than your own employees who know exactly how to make things operate more efficiently.

For example, even before the *Undercover Boss* show, from time to time I used to go and speak to drivers at 4:00 AM before they went out on their routes, to discuss safety, update them on how the company was doing and what we were focused on operationally, answer their questions, and ask them for their input on how we could improve our service to our customers and remove the things that caused them daily frustrations.

I would then pick one driver at random and tell him or her I was going to be their helper and work the back of their truck for the day. The last thing I wanted them to do was to go back to the shop at the end of the day and tell everyone what a terrible and lazy worker I was! I guess my upbringing in my family's construction business helped me learn to work hard and not be afraid to get my hands dirty!

Some people asked me why I would waste an entire day picking up trash on the back of a garbage truck, given my senior executive position with the company. My response was that I learned more about what was working and what wasn't, what was causing our employees unnecessary frustration, and how to respond to our customers more effectively by spending the day with our employees servicing our customers than by sitting in my ivory tower corporate office downtown.

I can't tell you how many times people told me no one from the corporate office had ever even been to their district before. I traveled more than two hundred days a year visiting our operations and customers, and wherever I went, I always made a point to go office to office, department to department, and cubical to cubical to visit with as many employees individually as I could. I never saw a frontline employee hesitate to tell me what was on their mind.

The employees I worked with provided me great suggestions and insight I otherwise would not have heard if I had not met with them in person. Spending an entire day with them, showing them how much I appreciated what they were doing, and learning what they thought we could do to improve gave them a voice. I always responded to each idea and suggestion. If it was a good idea, we implemented it. If it was not such a great idea, or something we couldn't implement at that time, I would explain why. They appreciated someone listening to them, seeking their input, and following up with them on their suggestions, even if we didn't implement them at the time.

Another thing happened from doing that. It got around the company. People began to trust us. The employees saw we not only valued their opinions, but we implemented many of them! We made clear throughout the organization the changes we were implementing were from individual employees, and we were listening. We recognized those employees and gave them the credit. And since it was the employees' ideas we wanted to implement, we gained immediate buy-in and ownership of the solution by the employees. It was their solution, not mine or the corporate office's solution.

This gave the employees a sense that this was about them, not just the leaders of the company. They had a feeling of sharing the power. It gave the team a sense that we are all in this together, rather than I work for her, or he works for me. It became all about *us*, not about the leaders. It was powerful indeed! It also showed the employees their leader would never ask them to do something their leader was not willing to do, and we cared.

One of the reasons the creators of the *Undercover Boss* hit television show wanted me to be in the premier episode was because they saw we were already listening to our employees at Waste Management to gain their insight for solutions to help turn our company around. The point they were trying to expose was how seldom that occurs in many businesses today. That got their attention when they heard about it, although it was something my dad trained me to do at an early age.

Approached by Undercover Boss *Show*

When the *Undercover Boss* show producers were looking for companies for the first pilot show, they reached out to one of the largest public relations firms in the U.S. to inquire whether any of their clients might have an interest. It just so happened we were using the same firm at Waste Management to help us restore our reputation after the prior management drove Waste Management into the ditch. I knew several of the principals at the firm through our work with them. They told the *Undercover Boss* producers they knew just the company (Waste Management) and just the guy (the principals knew I went out and worked with our frontline employees), but it would be difficult to convince him to do the show as he was private and not interested in calling attention to himself.

When the *Undercover Boss* producers learned I was going out working with the frontline employees, they were intrigued. They had a general idea of what they were trying to show the audience about bosses being out of touch, but they weren't sure how the show was all going to come together.

As they learned more about how we were listening to our employees, and from time to time I was already going out into our operations with my sleeves rolled up working the jobs side by side with the frontline employees and learning about their issues (I wasn't going undercover—the Waste Management employees knew who I was), they wanted me to do the first episode. The *Undercover Boss* folks thought it would be better to have someone like me, who was comfortable doing the frontline jobs, to film the pilot episode for the show, to help them see how the first show could come together.

When our team first brought this opportunity to me, I told them there was no way I was going to do a reality television show. I told them I don't even watch reality television. The little bit I knew about reality television was it appeared to me to be mostly about all the character flaws of the people on the show, and I told them I preferred to keep my character flaws to myself!

The producers told me the show was geared to bring out the personal stories of some of our great employees, and I knew our employees had those great stories from my experience working side by side with them. Our marketing department thought it would be great for the company to show everyone the wonderful quality of our frontline employees. That sounded good to me.

The problem was, the producers told us we would not have any editing rights. I was concerned about that. We had come such a long way in rebuilding our brand and our reputation, and I didn't know how the producers might put this film together. We took it to our board of directors, and they said on the one hand it could be beneficial for the company, yet on the other hand it could go terribly wrong. We hope you make the right decision!

We ultimately decided to do the show, as the producers told us we would be the pilot episode, and they were going to use our episode to attract other companies to film for the entire season before our episode even aired. I figured if they threw us under the bus, then no other company was going to be willing to do the show. So we decided to go ahead with the filming.

We told the employees a documentary film crew wanted to film a new employee's first day of work at Waste Management. Two guys with handheld cameras followed me around and filmed us as I did a different job working with new employees at a different location each day for about two weeks. The film crew never stopped us as we worked so that they could shoot from a different angle, and never asked us to do anything over so they could get us to say the same thing over again or in a different way. There were no scripts or rehearsals. They just filmed us as we worked, and we quickly forgot they were even filming us as we went about our work all day.

The *Undercover Boss* producers sought us out because they thought it was so unusual we were actually listening to our employees! We made clear to our employees we wanted ideas and suggestions from everyone in the company. I made sure our employees knew my email address, and I was accessible. I always tried to respond to every email and voice mail the same day and no later than the following day.

I also filmed short videos that played in break rooms across the company to keep employees up-to-date on what we were doing, tell them how they could contribute to our progress, share with them whose suggestions we were now implementing, and ask for their ideas.

We implemented so many great ideas we received from our employees. They included things like how we could make the check-in and check-out procedures for our drivers in the morning and evenings more efficient; how the drivers could alert the mechanics to problems they were beginning to have with their trucks so the mechanics could fix the problem over-night and we could avoid breakdowns on the road or delays in getting out on the route the next morning; how the mechanics could leave a note for the driver describing what they fixed the prior night, and if the work was not completed due to waiting on a part, when the repair was expected to be completed; ways to make our routes more efficient; how the drivers could report potentially unsafe container locations so we could have the container moved to a different location to avoid overhead wires and other unsafe situations; and how drivers could report where they were unable to service a location so we could proactively contact the customer electronically to tell them when we would return, eliminating the need for the customer to call into our call centers. These were just a few of the ideas we implemented that came from the operations personnel to improve our safety, efficiency, and performance.

I have not always gotten it right. For instance, during the filming of *Undercover Boss*, I learned for the first time while

I was out on a route serving as a helper for Janice our driver, that the process we put in place for our managers to conduct observations on their drivers to help coach them was viewed by some drivers as a spying initiative to catch them doing something wrong to fire them. I knew that was not the purpose of observations at all. That was a process I championed, and it is mentioned on the *Undercover Boss* episode.

The purpose of the process was to help our drivers with coaching and identifying things on their routes that were creating difficulties we could eliminate (like a container being placed in a location that was difficult to service when it could be moved to a different location to make it easier and safer for the driver). We were able to make some changes to the observation process based on what I learned from our drivers to make it more effective, beneficial, and appreciated by everyone.

Ask the Right Questions

A part of the characteristic of listening is for the servant leader to learn to ask the right questions to their team that can inspire new thinking. Sometimes leaders are afraid to ask questions when they don't know the answer because they don't want to appear ignorant. They want people to think they know it all.

Jesus told us to be lowly servants, and so I have never worried about asking a question when I don't know the answer. I guess I have always possessed an inquisitive mind, and I like to learn new things by asking questions. I also learned from some great leaders, who showed me that being willing to ask great questions not only shows the team you are engaged and interested in learning more about their operations and struggles, but it can also lead to some new thinking and tremendous opportunities.

Jim Woods, my mentor and retired chairman and CEO of Baker Hughes, mentioned in chapter 1, was a master at asking just the right questions. His instinct was amazing. He could walk into a conference room where the leadership team was meeting. We may have been meeting over an hour before he arrived, discussing various alternatives to a particular problem or opportunity.

Jim would sit down and listen to our discussion for a couple of minutes, and ask a couple of great questions, and then get up and walk away. I can't tell you how many times Jim's great questions caused us to see exactly what we needed to do. We may have been wrestling with a particular issue for a while, and yet the questions Jim asked focused our discussions and led us to the right solution. What a gift he had!

Asking great questions can at first make you feel vulnerable as a leader because you may be asking a question everyone but you knows the answer. I have found asking the right questions can lead to opportunities that might not otherwise be considered.

When I first arrived at Waste Management, I went out to look at one of our landfills, as I had never been to a landfill before, and I knew little about how a landfill actually operated. When I first arrived, I was intrigued to see the huge flare that was burning off methane gas from the landfill. As trash decomposes, it generates methane gas. If you have ever put grass cuttings into a plastic bag and then let the bag sit in the sun for a while, methane gas can be generated and sometimes even heat.

A gas flare is a tall pipe erected vertically into the air from underground within the landfill, and it has an ignition system at the top of the pipe so the methane gas is burned (flared) and consumed rather than being released into the atmosphere.

I studied structural engineering, soil mechanics, geology, and environmental engineering in college; and during my time at Baker Hughes, I acquired knowledge about early process systems/generators that ran on gas being produced at the wellhead in the oilfield. I saw some of the wellhead gas used to power camps, platforms, and drilling operations in the oilfield rather than being flared.

I was curious as to why they were flaring the gas and not putting it to some beneficial use. So I asked the management team to tell me about that big flare. They explained that as trash decomposes, it creates methane gas, and the environmental regulations require they flare the methane gas rather than let it just escape into the atmosphere. I told them I realized methane gas was produced from the decomposing trash. I acknowledged I should have asked my question better.

So I then asked why the gas was being flared rather than used for something beneficial. I said it looked like a huge flare (it was a large landfill), and it seemed to me with that much gas there must be some beneficial use that could be made of the gas. I told them I had no idea that much gas was created at a landfill because that was my first landfill to visit, and maybe I was just asking a stupid question. I told them I knew there were engines and generators that could run on poor qualities of gas. I asked if they ever looked into generating electricity or other beneficial uses of the gas.

The landfill team told me they converted landfill gas to energy at a few landfills in the company, but it was not a priority for the company, as they were focused on the trash coming into the landfill and building the landfill out in a safe and responsible manner. That is when I turned to the team traveling with me and said, "Wow, we just might be able to turn this company into an energy company!"

Well, that one question led us to create a landfill gas to energy group in the company responsible for installing and operating landfill gas to energy systems (electricity generation) at our landfills. This not only created an additional revenue stream, but it also turned the landfills into an energy resource!

We also developed a way to turn the landfill gas into liquefied natural gas (LNG) at one of our California landfills so we could fill up our trucks with LNG to run on rather than diesel fuel. This approach helped support our goal of recycling those things that made economic sense to recycle (where there was a viable market for the recycled material) and then create energy from those things sent to the landfill.

Empowerment not only enables your team to feel you are sharing the power with them. It also builds trust and can lead to some fantastic opportunities as you ask the right questions as the servant leader, empower your team to embark into unchartered territory, and listen to their response!

Many employees brought forth great ideas and helped us build the operating model that helped propel Waste

Management forward. When you don't listen to your employees or your teammates, and fail to empower them, you are wasting a tremendous opportunity to make a difference. You are passing by some great ideas and most likely missing the opportunity to create a culture of engaged employees.

Your employees can tell you many ideas to make your team better. When you listen to them and eliminate the things that cause them the most frustration in their job, you are on the way to a high-performing team! Jesus tells us to listen, and I found listening to your team is of vital importance to anyone who wants to be a respected servant leader making a difference in the lives of others. To do otherwise is simply *management waste*!

Commitment
Listening
Empathy
Accountability
Notice

Game Changer

Empathy

THE THIRD characteristic of servant leadership is *empathy*. Brené Brown—the researcher and author who has spent the past two decades studying courage, vulnerability, shame, and empathy—has said, "Empathy doesn't require we have the exact same experiences as the person sharing their story with us. . . . Empathy is connecting with the emotion that someone is experiencing, not the event or the circumstance."[1]

The apostle Paul tells us: "Do nothing out of selfish ambition or vain conceit. Rather, in humility value others above yourselves, not looking to your own interests but each of you to the interests of the others. In your relationships with one another, have the same mindset as Christ Jesus: Who, being in very nature God, did not consider equality with God something to be used to his own advantage; rather, he made

---

1. Brené Brown in Sophia Seltenreich, "The Key to Unlocking Empathy in Sales," Yesware, accessed August 28, 2020, https://www.yesware.com/blog/sales-empathy-2/Brown, Brene, About tab at www.brenebrown.com/about.

himself nothing by taking the very nature of a servant, being made in human likeness" (Philippians 2:3–7).

We see Jesus, who was God, humbling Himself to become not only a man but also a servant. Jesus cared about us so much that He gave His life to pay the debt of our sins so we could have eternal life with Him. Jesus exemplified the model of empathy and caring for others.

Jesus told us how important it is to love others and place their interests ahead of our own: "'Teacher, which is the greatest commandment in the Law?' Jesus replied: 'Love the Lord your God with all your heart and with all your soul and with all your mind.' This is the first and greatest commandment. And the second is like it: 'Love your neighbor as yourself'" (Matthew 22:36–39).

Henri Nouwen—internationally renowned priest, author, professor, who wrote thirty-nine books on the spiritual life—offered this definition of love in his book *The Road to Daybreak: A Spiritual Journey*: "When we honestly ask ourselves which person in our lives means the most to us, we often find that it is those who, instead of giving much advice, solutions, or cures, have chosen rather to share our pain and touch our wounds with a warm and tender hand."

Modeling Empathy

We can follow Jesus' command to us to love others as ourselves by demonstrating empathy to others—caring and having concern about others in a way you can sense their feelings to such an extent you share in their suffering. We are to live in a way that we have self-awareness of what is going on around us and in the lives of others, and then we put empathy into action to unlock our kindness and compassion to show we truly care and we have the love of Jesus Christ living within us.

Before God brought Linley into my life, I confess I had little empathy for others. While I was a Christian, I was still mainly self-absorbed and focused on me and my own plan rather than caring about others and focusing on God's plan. The shipwreck with Linley opened up a whole new world for me when God worked through her tragedy to teach me about empathy and what it truly means to care about others.

I am not going to tell you I have mastered empathy! I still fall into the trap of focusing on my own selfish desires rather than caring about others and seeking God's will and His plan. I still have plenty of work to do in this area, but I can tell you when I allow God to work through me as a servant leader, and I place others ahead of myself not only in business, but in all my relationships—relationships with colleagues, friends, family, and my wife—empathy changes everything!

When I can tap into empathy for others, people see I care about them, and I have genuine concern for them. As our trust in each other builds, it takes our relationship to an entirely new level. We both become more engaged with each other in our conversations, rather than just having superficial discussions about the weather and the latest items in the news or sports. We each begin to go out of our way to help the other. We begin to appreciate the things others do to help us or our team. And when other people have a struggle, it brings me joy to know I can encourage them and show them support through their struggle, as they in turn show how much they appreciate my encouragement and support.

Empathy is a game changer in any relationship. When a team is made up of people who have empathy for one another and fully support and care about one another, now you have the special ingredient for a high performance and winning team!

Everyone on our team at Waste Management worked really hard, and we sometimes worked long hours. I have always felt weekends should be mainly spent with family. Sure, it is necessary to work on weekends sometimes, but it should not be all weekend, every weekend, or something is terribly wrong.

One way I tried to model for our team was to make sure my cell phone number was readily available throughout the company. I made sure if people needed to speak with me on the weekend, they were to call me on my cell phone. I wanted them to know I cared about them, and if they needed me, I would always be there for them.

I also told them if they sent me an email on the weekend, they should not expect a response until Monday. It was not because I didn't want to hear from my team on the weekend. I cared about them and wanted them to spend time with their families. I did not want people sending me an email and then sitting by their cell phone or computer all weekend waiting for my response so they could send me a quick follow-up to show me they were working.

I also made clear that no one was coming around the office on the weekends to see if they were working. At one point I even considered shutting down the email system on the weekends! But my team convinced me not to do this since our business operated on weekends and holidays. They said they understood my point.

I tried to show I cared about them, and I wanted them to spend weekends focused on their family, and I was going to be doing the same. But if they really needed me, I told them not to hesitate to call me on my cell phone. I told them I know emergencies can come up on weekends, holidays, and late at night when you are working in a business that operates twenty-four hours a day, seven days a week, and I would always be available for them.

I tried hard to let all our employees see I felt a tremendous sense of responsibility for them and their families. I wanted them to see how important my family is to me, so they would know I also felt it was important for them to spend time with their own families on the days they had off. I think people felt appreciated and saw by my actions I cared about them and their families.

For a while I even changed my out-of-office assistant automatic reply on the email system when I left the office on Friday for the weekend to say I was spending the weekend with my family and they should not expect a response prior to Monday, but if they needed me during the weekend or if they were a customer, to please call me on my cell phone and I provided my cell phone number.

Empathy and caring about others also means making yourself vulnerable. Opening yourself up with others to share your own struggles helps build trust.

As I explained in chapter 1, when I first arrived at Waste Management, it was a disaster. The prior management acquired more than a thousand companies around the world, and these companies had not been put together well. Essentially, there was no single culture, as many of the companies were operating independently.

While I did a lot of due diligence before I decided to come on board to help build the new management team at Waste Management, help restore the integrity of the company and help begin the turnaround, one thing I did not realize was how bad their safety record was. And it was not just Waste Management that had a poor safety record; it was the entire industry.

As a $13.5 billion company, you wouldn't expect things to be so messed up. But it was like a $13.5 billion start-up company with no single operating system for all locations to use, no single financial system for everyone to use, no single culture, and definitely no safety culture.

As best as I could tell from the terrible records that existed when I first got there, our TRIR (Total Recordable Incident Rate) was in the mid-twenties (which for those of you who do not follow safety metrics, this was an industry with lots of safety incidents). People were getting injured often or even killed.

I will never forget asking a group of managers, when I first got there, about why they thought we experienced so many accidents and injuries. Their answer was that it was just the nature of the business. They told me we put twenty-five thousand trucks on the road every day, they were big trucks, and if someone came into contact with one of our trucks, they were going to get hurt.

They said I just didn't understand because I came from the oilfield, which is a safe industry. They obviously didn't understand the hazards of the oilfield, and the focus of companies in the oilfield industry to minimize accidents and injuries.

So I responded, "You are right. I know nothing about this industry. I need your help in understanding. Let me see if I follow what you are saying. We have a truck, and it runs a route all day, going from point A to point B, and we fill it up with trash along the way. But by the time it gets to the landfill, somebody is going to get injured somewhere in the company. Do I have that correct?"

They said yes, that is generally the way it works. So I continued, "OK, so now when I think about another industry that has vehicles that go from Point A to Point B, they fill up their vehicles with people instead of trash, and then they levitate the vehicle off the ground at about forty thousand feet during the route, and when they get to Point B at the end of the route, it is extremely rare for anyone to get hurt, much less killed. Why is that?" Of course, they knew I was talking about the airline industry, and they had no answer to my question.

A few days later I learned one of our employees lost his arm in some of our recycling equipment at one of our recycling processing centers. When I went to the facility to ask what happened, the employees told me, "Oh, that crazy Phillip. He did that all the time. When the recycling conveyor belt would get clogged with trash, he would just stick his arm in the shoot to clear it out while it was still running!" When

I asked the other employees why they hadn't said something to Phillip to warn him of the dangers, they looked at me like I was crazy—like why would we do that?

Need for Culture Change

We clearly had a problem. It wasn't a safety problem. We had a culture problem. A safety program was not going to solve our problem.

Some people had even lost their lives, and I made a priority to go speak to their families immediately. At first our lawyers weren't thrilled about my doing that. I told them it wasn't about whose fault it was; it was about showing the family how much we cared about them, regardless of whose fault it was. The fault and liability would get sorted out, but a life was now gone, some people were hurting, and we needed to show them empathy. We needed to show them we cared.

I never got comfortable talking to those families, and I think I cried with the family every time I spoke to a family following a fatality. It really impacted me, and I became determined to do whatever I could do to help eliminate all the accidents and injuries at our company.

I knew we had to get people to wake up and see the value of life rather than taking life for granted. I needed to help them see that when one person gets injured, it is not just the injured person who is affected; it impacts the entire family unit. Just like in my own family with Linley—we have all been impacted by the preventable mistake made by the doctor.

I wanted our culture to change and get to a place where people weren't just concerned about their own safety;

they were concerned about the safety of the people around them as well. A culture where when someone saw another employee about to do something unsafe, like stick their arm inside a conveyor while it was operating, or wearing their safety glasses on top of their head rather than over their eyes, they would stop and tell the person they care about their safety, and the person they told would actually thank them for caring and saying something to them.

I decided I needed to make myself vulnerable to help get the attention of our employees to show them what I learned about empathy and caring for others through my shipwreck with Linley. I thought by making myself vulnerable, and explaining how I learned about empathy and caring about the lives of others, and just how precious life really is, we might be able to begin to change our culture (along with the other things we were doing).

We started our culture change, naming it Mission to Zero with a logo M2Z. Our mission was to have zero incidents and injuries. But it couldn't just be a program. We needed to get to people's hearts. It needed to be in our DNA. It needed to start at the top with all of our leaders, and it needed to be everyone's mission, not just the safety department. Every manager and every employee had to own this. We needed to make it personal and make it everyone's responsibility. Safety can't be delegated. We needed buy-in, and we needed to build a culture where people had empathy for others.

We were in a crisis, and we needed a wake-up call. I started traveling to our operations and telling our drivers, mechanics, sorters, and managers about my shipwreck story with Linley. It was not easy for me to share Linley's story, and it still isn't. I wanted them to see how precious life is and how lives can be changed in an instant with a tragedy that can impact the entire family unit.

Sharing Linley's story was just one of the many things we did to help change our culture. I can't tell you how many times I saw some big, tough-looking guys, with tears in their eyes as I told Linley's story.

Don't get me wrong, I am not taking credit for the incredible change in our safety culture. A lot of talented people and safety professionals embraced what we were trying to do and joined together to lead the dramatic change in our safety DNA through the many aspects of our campaign to change our safety culture and help people discover the empathy tool in their own toolbox.

All of us who shared our personal stories showed vulnerability, which helped build trust at every level of our team. I would tell the story about the negative impacts that resulted because one doctor's action led to catastrophic results. He didn't intend to cause harm, but he didn't take the time to ask how to do the procedure on a three-month-old infant, having done the procedure only on adults previously.

I told them about all the needless pain, suffering, brain damage, and impacted lives that resulted because he didn't take the time to stop and ask a few simple questions before proceeding with the wrong instrument, leaving our precious three-month-old daughter with severe brain damage and causing immense trauma throughout our entire family.

He didn't take the time to ask, "How is this situation different from what I typically encounter? I have always done this on adults. What should be done differently with a three-month-old infant? Are instruments and techniques the same or different?"

Please, don't misunderstand me—I know the doctor did not intentionally cause my daughter's brain damage, and I have forgiven him. But I want you to see how important it is to take the time to ask yourself what is different when you encounter a new situation. Before assuming a situation is the same as usual, consider possible outcomes. Lack of thought and proper planning can result in permanent, irreversible consequences, and maybe even death. Safety and watching out for others has to be at the forefront of your thinking all the time. It has to become part of your DNA.

We started having the children of our drivers write notes to their mom or dad who worked for us as a driver to tell them how much they loved their parents and to ask them to be safe so they could see them at home that night after work. The idea was to get people to think about their own safety and about caring for their family. How would their family cope if they were killed because they got in a hurry, cut corners, or did something unsafe.

We educated people on eye injuries, which are serious are also the easiest injury to prevent. You just have to wear safety glasses. How many of you operate your Weed Eater and don't wear safety glasses? I can't believe I used to do that! How crazy to go out and shoot rocks up at your unprotected eyes!

We recognized and promoted the reporting of unsafe situations workers encountered along their routes so we could make them safer. We established a system to report any near misses so we could make adjustments. Our view was a near miss was just lucky. That mailbox our truck backed into could have been a child. With a near-miss report like that, we would look at how to change the route to eliminate the backup maneuver.

We even reconfigured our routes to eliminate left-hand turns (which are not only dangerous but also add to route time as drivers waited to turn across oncoming traffic).

We created Life Critical Rules—ten rules for our drivers that were not optional. The Life Critical Rules included:

1. Never back up a vehicle with someone on the riding steps at the back of the vehicle.
2. Never exceed the speed limits posted or set by policy for school zones, riding steps, and stand-up right-side driving.
3. Always comply with seat belt rules.
4. Never modify or disable equipment safety devices.
5. Always apply parking brakes when exiting a vehicle to prevent the vehicle from rolling away.

Employees who didn't comply with the Life Critical Rules were putting their own life or the lives of those around them at risk, and we let them go work elsewhere. We let them leave to go to work in a culture that didn't value life and didn't value empathy.

We reviewed every accident we experienced, determined the root cause (how we could have prevented the incident), and reported it throughout the company so everyone could learn from the incident and do their part to keep it from happening again.

We created our own Driving Science Series videos that played in our breakrooms. We filmed our trucks and our employees, including me, to teach safe driving and operating practices. Using our own people and equipment rather than actors and off-the-shelf canned safety films for these videos resonated with our team and drove home the importance of safe operating practices.

We conducted safety observations for our drivers. These were not "gotcha" sessions, as I mentioned in chapter 4, but sessions to observe our employees going about their job, followed by coaching sessions to discuss ways they could do their jobs safer.

In some cases we learned we needed to move a container to a safer location for servicing to reduce the risk of an accident. The employees quickly learned we were all in this together, and the observation process was intended to help them rather than to catch them doing things wrong.

We taught our managers this was an opportunity for them to show their leadership and to serve others. We told them not to think of themselves as the police but as a coach who cared about their team. As long as you think of yourself as a resource to serve those in your charge, people will want to follow you because they know you care about them. You have the authority to force others to follow the rules of the company, but without inspiration, what do you think they will do when you turn your back?

We made clear, of all their contributions to the company, nothing is more important than their impact on the safety culture. Safety is about caring for others and saving lives—a true mark of a team that knows how to live their lives with empathy.

In his book *Management: Tasks, Responsibilities, Practices*, Peter Drucker, a renowned management consultant, once said, "Leadership is not magnetic personality. . . . It is not 'making friends and influencing people.' . . . Leadership is lifting a person's vision to higher sights, the building of a person's performance to a higher standard."

I used to tell our leaders, before you decide an individual does not have what it takes to be part of our team, first examine your own heart and ask if you have exhausted your capacity to teach them and care for them. I asked managers to ask themselves before they fired someone, "Did that employee fail us, or did we fail them by not telling them clearly our expectations, providing them the training and the tools they need to succeed, and showing them empathy by coaching them along the way?"

To have a great team, leaders need first to examine themselves and begin their own transformation. Safety needs to be personal, and they needed to tell their own story to their team (like my story about my daughter), to get people to realize the importance of safety and caring about others. Everyone has a personal story they can use to connect with their team. I encouraged them to let their actions show they knew how to put empathy into action, and if they modeled that behavior, the rest of their team would follow.

Jesus continually told us to love one another. Jesus said, "By this everyone will know that you are my disciples, if you love one another" (John 13:35). You might be familiar with the song, "They'll Know We Are Christians." How will people know we are Christians? By our love!

So my question to you is this: Do the people you work with know you are a Christian because of the love, care, and empathy you show to them? If I went to your business and took a survey, what would they say about you? Would they tell me they know you are a Christian by the empathy you show them?

We probably all have work to do with regard to empathy. You may have heard someone say, "People will seldom remember what you said, but they will always remember how you made them feel." That has always stuck with me, and it is something I continually think about when I am trying to show empathy to others.

While our culture may expect us to leave God at home or in the car when we come to work, God wants us to show others by our words and actions each day that we are indeed Christians, and we have the Holy Spirit living inside of us.

The apostle Peter tells us, "All of you, be like-minded, be sympathetic, love one another, be compassionate and humble" (1 Peter 3:8). The apostle Paul tells us to "rejoice with those who rejoice; mourn with those who mourn" (Romans 12:15); "encourage one another and build each other up" (1 Thessalonians 5:11); and "carry each other's burdens, and in this way you will fulfill the law of Christ [to love one another]" (Galatians 6:2).

By unlocking empathy with others, encouraging them, and helping them when they are down, we show them how much we care about them. Empathy is a powerful tool when it is deployed, and shows us to be the type of loving person

God intended us to be. We each get to choose what type of leader we want to be. How will your team remember you?

Life Changer

I will never forget meeting with the wife and kids of a man who had been killed on the freeway by a Waste Management driver who lost control of his truck. I met with them just after the tragic accident, and what was really sad was the accident could have been prevented. I remember crying with all of them and telling them how sorry I was.

What an amazing lady the wife is. She ended up wanting to help us use the incident in a way to save lives. She helped us kick off a program we called Life Changer. She told her story of how her life and her kids' lives were impacted by the loss of her husband, and her kids told about how tough it was to have lost their dad.

We then started recognizing people each year with our Life Changer Award, people who did something to save lives and positively impact others in a significant way that year. These were people who modeled empathy. Their stories also helped us change the culture throughout the company. It made safety personal, not a program. People were beginning to see that they needed to change their hearts and appreciate how precious life is. They needed to tap into empathy as they discovered how powerful a tool it can be.

Safety at Waste Management wasn't a program; it became our way of life, our DNA. A strong safety culture driven by empathy not only helped shape our company, but it brought us all together as a team.

I want to share one additional story with you to illustrate how you can demonstrate empathy to your own family and show them by your own actions how much you care about them.

I remember the reaction I first got when I made the announcement at Waste Management that nobody could use their cell phones (talking, texting, or even hands-free) while they were driving. We were still having too many accidents that were being caused by distracted driving—using cell phones while driving. This was back in the early 2000s when everyone was talking and texting while driving.

That announcement was not well received in the company. I thought everyone was either going to quit or kill me. So I started going around to each of our facilities and telling all our employees again about Linley's tragic accident and how precious life is. And then I would tell them this story (and please read the following as if I am speaking directly to you):

> I want you to think right now of the person you love the most. It might be your wife, a child, a parent, a sibling, a boyfriend or girlfriend. Somebody you love more than anyone else in the world. Now do you have that person's face in your mind? OK, let's just say right after we conclude our talk (or your reading of this chapter), you get a phone call and hear your loved one has just been killed in a terrible car accident. The person driving the other car was talking or

texting on the phone and was distracted, and now your loved one is gone. You will never see them again. How would you feel? How would you cope? How would you get by? How would your life be forever changed by not having that person in your life anymore?

Now let's change it up a bit. What if *you* were the one driving and you killed the other person because you were distracted while you were talking on your cell phone? How would you feel? How would you live with yourself knowing what you just did to that person and their family? Don't read on until you have truly reflected on that.

OK, now bring back into your mind the loved one you were just thinking of. If you really love that person, or you love the rest of your family (or maybe you have high school or college kids who are driving now), I hope as soon as you get home (or finish reading this chapter), you will sit down with them and tell them you have decided to make a big change in your life because you care about them so much. You have decided you are not going to talk or text while driving anymore, and you love them so much you don't want them to talk or text while driving either. You want to see them again.

I care about my family and all my friends so much, and I am so serious about not talking (even hands-free) or texting

Chapter 5. Game Changer

on my cell phone while driving, the auto reply on my cell phone voice mail says, "I am sorry I can't talk to you right now. I am either on the phone, in a meeting, or driving, and I will call you back as soon as I get free." My friends and family know I will not talk to them if they call me while they are driving in their car.

If someone calls me and I sense they are driving in their car, I will politely tell them to call me back when they are stopped. I do not want to be the last person they talked to just before killing themselves because they are distracted by talking to me on the phone. I don't want to live with that burden on my heart.

If you love your family, please make a commitment right now to change your own behavior and demonstrate empathy and how much you care for your own family and friends. Commit today to stop talking and texting while driving. Do you really think your family can make it without you? And if you want to continue to see each of your family members every day, and you really love them, please talk to them about not talking or texting while driving.

I know not everyone reading this book is going to heed my plea. People are killed every day by distracted driving. Today we have the statistics that show the dangers of talking and texting on your cell phone while driving. Just look around you next time you are on the freeway at how many people are texting while driving. If you are talking and/or texting on your phone, I fear for you—it is not a matter of *if*, it is just a matter of *when*.

I hope this chapter has not only started you thinking more about your own empathy as a servant leader but has

87

also started you thinking about caring more for your own family and the people you work with. Once our team at Waste Management began to tap into empathy, it was a game changer. While it brought about a tremendous impact on our safety, it even positively impacted our overall performance.

As people began to sincerely care about one another, teams came together, and new bonds of friendship were formed. People volunteered to help one another. A sense of being on a winning team developed, and we were all in this together. People wanted to be there and contribute to the team's success. There was a sense of camaraderie.

We even began measuring employee engagement within the company, and we saw marked improvement in how engaged our employees were at each level of the organization as employees discovered the magic of empathy.

Empathy changes everything. That discovery (and its revelation by God through my shipwreck with Linley) changed my life. When you care about others, what comes back to you is way more than what you put into it. It is more joyful to give than to receive. I think that is why Jesus told us to love others. When we tap into empathy for others, it is the magic that can take our relationships with our spouse, family, friends, and coworkers to a whole new level, and bring a tremendous sense of joy to our lives.

Commitment
Listening
Empathy
Accountability
Notice

CHAPTER 6

The Loneliest Job in the World
Accountability

T HIS MAY be surprising to some of you, but ascending to a level of leadership can become one of the loneliest positions you will ever have. When everyone is looking to you to lead them, you may feel like you have no one to turn to for wise counsel or to bounce ideas off of before sharing your ideas with your team. In times of stress or challenges, being a leader can be lonely because you have a sense of tremendous *accountability* to and responsibility for the people on your team, and yet you have nobody you feel you can talk to.

I think everyone in leadership needs a coach/mentor. I also believe every Christian needs a spiritual coach/leader (I will discuss that later in this chapter).

Even Jesus, who is God, sought out and followed the instructions of God the Father. Jesus tells us, "Very truly I tell you, the Son can do nothing by himself; he can do only what he sees his Father doing, because whatever the Father does the Son also does" (John 5:19). So even Jesus, who is God and

Lord, continually sought the will of God the Father and only did what God the Father showed Him to do.

We are to do the same in our roles as servant leaders. The apostle Paul tells us, "In your relationships with one another, have the same mindset as Christ Jesus: Who, being in very nature God, did not consider equality with God something to be used to his own advantage; rather, he made himself nothing by taking the very nature of a servant, being made in human likeness" (Philippians 2:5–7).

Jesus, who is God, did not come to earth to be served by man, but rather He came to earth to seek and carry out the will of God the Father and serve others. Jesus held Himself accountable to do the will of the Father and did what the Father showed Him to do.

I believe leaders who have been under authority make better leaders than those who have not. As Christians, we are to be committed to being under God's authority. It is *management waste* to be placed into a position of authority and then not be willing to submit to God's authority and follow God's design of servant leadership in our position of authority.

Have you ever tried to help a friend or a child by telling them how to avoid a problem you have experienced in your life, but then they just ignore you? How does that make you feel? Just think how God must feel when we refuse to follow His teaching in the Bible or we fail to learn what He is teaching us through our trials. The good news is God never gives up on us. He says, "And surely I am with you always, to the very end of the age" (Matthew 28:20).

Even Jesus, who is God, never claimed God's authority over others. Jesus submitted to God's will and said He was here to do God's will. "For I have come down from heaven not to do my will but to do the will of him who sent me" (John 6:38). In our roles as Christian leaders, we should continually seek out the will of God, recognizing that it is God who has put us in our roles, and He has a plan for us in our roles. We must be accountable to God's authority rather than relying on ourselves, or we will surely fail as leaders.

In this chapter we will look at the need for coaches and mentors in our lives as leaders to help us continue to grow and develop, to bounce ideas off of, and to hold us accountable to develop as servant leaders.

Talking to God

Let me first remind us as Christians: we now have direct access to God the Father through His Son Jesus, and by the power of the Holy Spirit who dwells within us. We are told, "If any of you lacks wisdom, you should ask God, who gives generously to all without finding fault, and it will be given to you" (James 1:5). So as servant leaders, we should always ask God to give us wisdom. We see Jesus often withdrawing from the disciples to go and pray to God the Father: "But Jesus often withdrew to lonely places and prayed" (Luke 5:16).

Jesus prayed before making big decisions, like before He chose the twelve disciples: "One of those days Jesus went out to a mountainside to pray, and spent the night praying to God. When morning came, he called his disciples to him and chose twelve of them, whom he also designated apostles" (Luke 6:12–13).

Jesus also showed us it is OK to pray to God the Father for what we want, but after telling the Father what we want, we should then tell the Father we want His will to be done, not ours. God wants a personal relationship with us, and He wants us to tell Him what is on our mind (even though He already knows) and then seek His will for our lives.

We see this modeled for us when Jesus prayed to God the Father before going to the cross, and Jesus asked the Father if it was possible He might not have to die such a horrible death on the cross, but the Father's will be done: "Going a little farther, he fell with his face to the ground and prayed, 'My Father, if it is possible, may this cup be taken from me. Yet not as I will, but as you will'" (Matthew 26:39).

The point I want to make here is it is OK to pray at work. I recognize prayer at work seems to be totally counter to our culture. But remember, Jesus prayed to God the Father all the time. So, why do we think we can't pray at work? If Jesus prayed to the Father before choosing His twelve disciples, wouldn't it be wise for us to follow His model and pray for wisdom before we make big decisions at work?

The book of James in the Bible tells us to pray to the Father for wisdom (James 1:5). God is always with us, and He wants a personal relationship with us. God wants us to communicate with Him and seek wisdom from Him continuously.

The apostle Paul tell us to pray continually, without ceasing (1 Thessalonians 5:17). I think this means we should pray throughout the day, even at work—in our office, walking down the hall on our way to a meeting, and while we are driving to and from work. I have found I seldom even turn on my car radio anymore, as my drive time when I am alone in the car gives me a great opportunity to communicate with and listen to God.

While you can find many opportunities to pray quietly at your desk at work, you may also become aware of appropriate times to pray with others at work. James tells us to pray for one another (James 5:16). An approach I have used from time to time is to ask my team if it is OK with them if I pray for us. That approach may not always be right for everyone's situation at work, and you should not make others uneasy or risk getting fired. I simply said that God is important to me so, do you mind if I pray for us? Few people ever voiced even the slightest objection or discomfort, and typically people appreciated those prayers. But again, you should not make anyone uncomfortable. You certainly should not force fellow employees to pray with you.

Sometimes, when I could tell by my conversation with a colleague they were going through a tough time outside of work or at home, I asked if I could pray for them or with them. Rarely did anyone refuse my offer to pray with them. In fact, just doing that has led to many opportunities to later share my faith with them. Sometimes it was weeks or months later they would ask me to tell them more about where I seemed to find peace in my life. The Bible tells us to always be prepared to give a reason to everyone who asks us to give the reason for the hope that is within us (1 Peter 3:15).

Mentoring, Coaching, and Discipling

I have been blessed to have several more experienced leaders help me throughout my career by being a leadership coach and mentor to me. I have also been blessed by a few people who are more advanced in their walk with Jesus Christ who have served as my discipleship coach. I previously mentioned Jim Woods, the former chairman and CEO of Baker Hughes, who served as a mentor to me for decades until he passed away recently.

When I was CEO, I sometimes felt alone as I struggled with making the right decision. I felt accountable to our employees, shareholders, and customers, and I didn't want to let them down. Jim was someone I could explain the situation to and describe the various options I was considering and what I saw were the pros and cons of each of those options. Jim, who was blessed with a gift for asking the right questions, would then ask me many questions that helped guide my thinking to arrive at the best solution.

Because Jim was not with my company at that time, he was not on my board of directors, and he was not my boss, his only desire was to help me make the best decision. Talking with him was a penalty-free environment for me to ask his thoughts without having to worry about his thinking I was asking stupid questions. Jim was only there as my friend and more experienced mentor, to help me succeed. He always helped me think through the situation more thoroughly, and he always left the decision up to me.

When you look at some of the best and most gifted athletes, they all have professional coaches to help them continue to improve and to talk with them about their game. A mentor is someone to help guide you and coach you. Someone to share your struggles with and to give you guidance and support, to help you deliver on your accountability to others.

Often the best people at being business mentors are those who are more experienced and have been through the battles, who can give you the insight and a different perspective you might not have. Someone who has been there and can understand what you may be going through, to help you navigate.

That is how Jim Woods was to me. I will always consider Jim a dear friend, and I miss him greatly. I learned a lot about leadership and business from Jim, and I am grateful for what he taught me, his guidance and mentoring throughout my career, and the opportunities he gave me at Baker Hughes to grow in my career.

If you don't have someone like that in your life, you need to find someone. I have felt so honored when others have asked me to serve as their business and/or spiritual mentor. So pray to God to help you find a mentor and then go ask the person if they would be willing to help mentor and coach you.

And then you need to be willing to be a mentor and coach to others. God calls us to make disciples of others (Matthew 28:19). A traditional concept used in medical schools to teach surgical skills is sometimes referred to as See One, Do One, Teach One. We can use the same technique, by having a mentor or coach to help us see how to do things differently and coach us through doing new things, and/or disciple us in our spiritual growth. Then we can in turn become a mentor or coach to teach and/or disciple others.

I have gotten so much joy out of mentoring, coaching, and discipling others. God places people in my life from time to time and leads me to help them. For example, I was introduced to a young man about a year or so ago by a mutual friend. My friend thought I might be able to help this young man who just started his business career by being a mentor to him.

When I first met this guy, I learned about some struggles he was having communicating with his boss. I listened to him, asked him a lot of questions to help him think through his situation, and over a period of months, he was able to improve the communication with his boss dramatically.

I continue to meet with him regularly, and he always comes to our meetings prepared with his questions and takes notes the entire time. He is very coachable, and it has been an absolute joy for me to watch him develop and succeed in his own career.

I also disciple about five to seven guys each year. I meet with each of them separately each week for about nine to twelve months. Before I even begin discipling someone, I tell him I am more than happy to spend the year discipling him, but he has to agree after the twelve months to then go and disciple others. As the apostle Paul tells us: "The things which you have heard from me in the presence of many witnesses, entrust these to faithful men who will be able to teach others also" (2 Timothy 2:2 NASB).

A great resource to use for discipling others is *The Four Priorities* by Dr. John Tolson and Larry Kreider. That book is a tool you can use to generate discussion. Everyone you disciple will be at a different point in their maturity as a Christian, and the important thing is to help them grow in their relationship with God and equip them to make disciples of others. That is what Jesus commanded each of us to do in Matthew 28:19–20.

I encourage you to give it a try with just one person this year. God may use you and work in and through you as part of His plan to change someone's eternity! Seeing the Lord work through you to help another person grow in relationship with God and equip them to become disciple makers will bring you tremendous joy.

Jesus as Mentor

I began this chapter by saying being a leader can sometimes feel very lonely, particularly when we are going through tough times. Just because we are Christians does not mean we will not have tough times and challenges in our lives. Jesus tells us, "In this world you will have trouble. But take heart! I have overcome the world" (John 16:33). So we know at the outset we are going to experience trials and struggles throughout our life.

Jesus also tells us He will be with us always (Matthew 28:20), even through our tough times. Jesus said, "Do not let your hearts be troubled. You believe in God; believe also in Me" (John 14:1).

While I don't have this perfected, the times in my career when I was going through a lonely time at work trying to sort through a particular challenge, I was able to find tremendous peace when I reflected back on my shipwreck with Linley.

First of all, through that reflection I realized God was indeed with me. The Holy Spirit was living in me as a Christian. I was able to remember God told me it is about *His* plan, not my plan, and I needed to trust Him. I then realized what I was struggling with at work was not a matter of life or death, and maybe God was trying to teach me something through this difficulty or inconvenience.

When I have been able to remember the Holy Spirit is right there living inside me, my entire disposition moves from being uptight to finding peace. Now, when I am facing a difficulty, I try to remember what the apostle Paul told us, "Do you not know that you are a temple of God and that the Spirit of God *dwells in you*?" (1 Corinthians 3:16 NASB; emphasis added).

Instead of being fearful, or being consumed with worry or distress over the situation, I try to remember to trust God, just as He told me in the Bible:

- "Be strong and courageous. Do not be afraid or terrified because of them, for the LORD your God goes with you; he will never leave you nor forsake you" (Deuteronomy 31:6).
- "God has said, 'Never will I leave you; never will I forsake you.' So we say with confidence, 'The Lord is my helper; I will not be afraid. What can mere mortals do to me?'" (Hebrews 13:5–6).

As servant leaders, we are to constantly seek the will of God for our lives and our team through our prayers. As Christians, we have an incredible mentor at our disposal— the Holy Spirit, living inside us. The Holy Spirit intercedes for us and makes our prayers sound beautiful to God the Father and helps us discern God's will for our lives: "In the same way, the Spirit helps us in our weakness. We do not know what we ought to pray for, but the Spirit himself intercedes for us through wordless groans. And he who searches our hearts knows the mind of the Spirit, because the Spirit intercedes for God's people [believers] in accordance with the will of God. And we know that in all things God works for the good of those who love him, who have been called according to his purpose" (Romans 8:26–28).

I have reflected many times on the story of Joseph in the Bible (Genesis 37–50) who totally trusted in God, even through his various times of difficulty. Joseph's brothers wanted to kill him because they thought Joseph was arrogant and they were also jealous because Joseph seemed to be their father's favorite son. Joseph's brothers decided, rather than killing Joseph, to capture him and sell him into slavery. They also sprinkled the varicolored tunic Joseph's father made for him with the blood of a male goat, to make his father believe a wild beast killed Joseph.

After being sold as a slave, Joseph ended up in Egypt and eventually became the personal servant of Potiphar, an official of Pharaoh in Egypt. The wife of Potiphar wanted to have sex with Joseph, but Joseph refused and held to his integrity and faith in God. Potiphar's wife was mad at Joseph for refusing her advances, so she accused Joseph of trying to have sex with her, and Joseph was placed in jail.

Joseph was later freed from jail because he could interpret Pharaoh's dreams. Eventually Joseph was promoted by Pharaoh to the position of prime minister of Egypt at age thirty, because God enabled Joseph to interpret one of Pharaoh's dreams. There would be a great famine, but there would be seven years of abundance before the famine. They could save and store grain before the famine. God essentially worked through Joseph to save all of Egypt.

I encourage you to read the entire story, because it is moving to see the way Joseph's family hears grain is available in Egypt during the famine (not knowing Joseph is there and is the one who is responsible for there being grain). Joseph's brothers travel to Egypt to get grain, and when they discover Joseph is now essentially acting as the prime minister of Egypt, they fear for their lives. But Joseph has compassion on his brothers and moves his entire family to Egypt to take care of them, saying his faith and trust in God allowed God to work good through his life where others (his brothers) intended evil.

What a great model Joseph is for us to trust in God, even in the face of evil, so we can allow God to work in us and through us to turn the evil into good. I can only imagine how lonely Joseph was after being sold as a slave and ending up alone in Egypt. Yet we never see Joseph complaining or crying out to God, saying life is not fair! At least some of Joseph's older brothers—Joseph had ten older brothers and one younger brother—should have been a mentor to him. Instead, they were the exact opposite. They were jealous of Joseph and sold him into slavery to get rid of him. So even though Joseph didn't have a human mentor in his life that we know about, Joseph continually sought out God's will for his life and trusted God as his mentor. God clearly worked through Joseph's life and trials in many ways.

We all go through difficult times in our lives, and we can feel lonely when we are struggling at work and don't have anyone to talk to about it. Jesus does not promise us a life on earth without difficult times. The apostle Paul tells us in Romans 5:3–5 that God will allow difficulties in our lives to build our character, strengthen our faith, draw us closer to Him, or for other reasons known only to God. Sometimes we won't fully understand the purpose of some of the difficulties we go through in our lives. But God asks us to place our faith in His Son Jesus.

God can take those difficult times in our lives and turn them into a positive to draw us closer to Him and sometimes to draw others closer to Him by seeing how we deal with our own problems with the help of the Holy Spirit. God sometimes reveals Himself to us and draws us closer to Him through our suffering in a personal way.

Jesus will always be with us, no matter how bad things may seem. If we just place our faith in Him, all will work out to bring glory to God. As God tells us in Isaiah 43:5, "Do not be afraid, for I am with you." Our Lord promises to meet us in the middle of whatever trouble we find ourselves in— whether a problem with our family relationships, a medical issue, financial difficulties, or problems at work. Jesus will meet us in the middle of the struggle to guide us through if we just trust Him. That is a promise you can rely on if you have placed your faith in His Son Jesus. There is no better mentor to have than to have a relationship with Jesus Christ. We can tap into the power of the Holy Spirit living inside of us as Christians.

Let me wrap up this chapter by taking you back to what I learned going through the trial with my daughter's medical accident. As I discussed in chapter 1, I was a Christian when my daughter's tragedy happened, and while I didn't lose my faith, I can tell you I became angry with God. I didn't curse God, but I told Him it was just not fair. I didn't understand why He would let this happen to us.

I had faith that God was able to cure our daughter and save us from this suffering, and I prayed that prayer what seemed like all day every day. I have never felt so alone and isolated. All I wanted to do was crawl into a hole and hope everything would just go away. At first, my faith was not strong enough to trust that God had this—that He had a plan. My focus was on myself and how unfair this was for God to let this happen to me and my precious two-month-old daughter.

Fortunately, through God's grace, God did give me the faith to keep praying to Him and reading my Bible throughout the suffering I was enduring. The Holy Spirit, my mentor, helped me finally see God did indeed have a different plan for my daughter—a plan that would bring Him glory. It is certainly different from the plan I had for my daughter, and there are still times of pain and suffering that she, my wife, and I all endure.

I don't have all the answers about why this happened to my daughter. But I can tell you I now have no doubt in my mind that God's plan has involved His working in and through my daughter in a way that has not only drawn me into a much closer relationship with God, but her life has been a huge positive impact on many other people. She is the most positive person you would ever want to meet given all her physical and mental disabilities. She is truly my inspiration!

It has taken me awhile to understand when I come upon tough times in my life, and I begin to pray to God to please keep me out of this difficulty or whatever the struggle is that I am then encountering. I now recognize that I am really asking God to keep me out of any pain, suffering, and inconvenience. And while I am not great at this yet, I now see when I pray like that, I may inadvertently be asking God to remove the opportunity He has placed before me that would enable me to grow in my faith and my relationship with Him by going through that trial.

I am now working on having unshakable faith like Joseph so I can face the difficulties and struggles in my life with conviction that God is with me, He has a plan, and He wants to teach me something through this struggle. Or He may be using my difficulty as a way for others to see the way God works in my life to help me face the struggle with positive conviction in Him that can then bring them closer to God. That causes me to pause and think about how others see my attitude when I encounter difficulties. Do I face my difficulties with the confidence I see in Joseph?

I certainly don't have this mastered yet, but I have definitely seen the difference in my own life when I face a difficult time or an inconvenience, to stop and say to Jesus, my mentor, "Jesus, I appreciate Your taking an interest in me today. What are You trying to teach me through this difficulty? Please use this event in a way to draw me closer to You. And please give me the strength to handle it in a way that draws others closer to You and bring You glory."

I know in my heart Jesus is there with me in the struggle! I have gotten closer to God when I take that approach and ask Him to join with me in the struggle to teach me and draw me closer, rather than asking Him to save me from the fire or the battle I am in. It is *management waste* for Christians, who have God living inside them, not to access Him and turn control over to Him.

I feel blessed that I learned at an early age that all roads do not lead to a personal relationship to God the Father. I would never have made it through the shipwreck with my daughter without my faith in Jesus Christ. If you are not a Christian, and you are interested in learning more about how I placed my faith in Jesus Christ, please turn to chapter 11.

Commitment
Listening
Empathy
Accountability
Notice

CHAPTER 7

"Dumbster"

Notice

THE FIFTH characteristic of servant leadership I want to discuss is *notice*. Being a servant leader means taking notice of the people around you rather than being so self-absorbed and focused on yourself. The apostle Paul tells us, "Do nothing out of selfish ambition or vain conceit. Rather, in humility value others above yourselves, not looking to your own interests but each of you to the interests of the others" (Philippians 2:3–4).

Taking notice of others means getting to know your colleagues on a personal basis, not just on a superficial level or being dumb when you are around the people you work with. *Dumb* means "being unable or unwilling to speak."

Putting notice into action means throwing your dumb muteness (your unwillingness to speak) into the trash dumpster and making an intentional effort to speak with others—not just small talk but really engaging with them and getting to know them by asking about their family, their hobbies, and personal interests. It means progressing the relationship with others to the point they are comfortable sharing personal joys and struggles with you.

The Power of Noticing

One of the people I worked with while I was undercover on the Waste Management *Undercover Boss* episode was named Jackie in upstate New York. I had never met and did not know Jackie before I was introduced to her as my new boss during that segment on the show. I immediately noticed Jackie had way too many jobs for one person. I knew our organizational structure was not set up for someone to have so many different roles simultaneously.

As I spent more time with Jackie, I learned there were several unfilled openings at that location, and she was just doing the best she could do to help keep the place running until the open positions could be filled. I also noticed Jackie never complained about her tremendous workload. She just got things done.

As I worked with Jackie that day, I was impressed with her positive attitude and work ethic, and I really wanted to get to know her on a personal level to better understand what drove her. As we talked throughout the day, I learned more about her and her family, and I discovered not only did many people depend on Jackie at work to get things done, but she also had tremendous family responsibilities at home. Her father had moved in with her, her husband, and daughter. Her sister and brother-in-law had recently moved in with them as well. Her brother-in-law had been recently discharged from the military and was looking for a job. A lot of people were depending on Jackie.

We spent the entire day working together, and if you watched the show, you saw she felt so sorry that I just arrived into town and, she assumed I didn't know anyone. To help welcome me to town, she invited me to dinner at her home that evening to meet her family.

When I arrived at her house, I noticed there was a for-sale sign out in the front yard. After she introduced me to her extended family, she showed me around her home. I noticed she kept referring to her home as her "dream home" and telling me she felt so blessed to have it.

When I asked her why it was for sale since it was her dream home, she told me the property taxes were going through the roof, and they could no longer afford to live there. I noticed she was upset thinking about having to leave her dream home she and her husband worked so hard for.

As I left her house after a beautiful evening with her family, Jackie's situation really weighed on me. Here we had this exemplary employee who loved our company and was working hard doing multiple jobs without complaint. She had a huge extended family depending on her, and she was about to lose her home. I just kept thinking about the situation that night after I left her house. I couldn't sleep thinking about her terrible situation at home.

I decided to risk breaking cover and being discovered during the filming of the *Undercover Boss* show. I arranged to meet with her supervisor, the district manager of her location whom I did know, to discuss Jackie's situation.

I told Jackie's supervisor I was the "new employee" Jackie had been working with, and we were the ones being filmed by the documentary crew filming "a new employee's first day at Waste Management." That is what we told everyone about the presence of the film crew.

I asked him to tell me what type of employee Jackie was, and he told me she had always been an exemplary employee. She was always the first to volunteer to help out anywhere she was needed. I had several discussions with him (both during and after the filming at her work location), and we determined that Jackie was so talented and capable that we needed to promote her to a higher position in the organization where she could fully use her skills. In fact, we promoted Jackie several more times during the following year or so after the filming of the show, and by the time I left Waste Management, she was serving as a sales manager.

Jackie deserved each of those promotions she received, and she and her husband were able to keep their home. I continued to stay in touch with her after I left Waste Management.

I share that story with you not because it was something special we did because of the *Undercover Boss* show but rather that was fairly typical of my visits to our various operating locations when I was not undercover for the filming of the *Undercover Boss* show. As I discussed in chapter 3 on commitment, I took notice of people as I toured our many operations around the world, and when I discovered people I felt were ready for a bigger role, I wrote their name down on the legal pad I always kept with me for that purpose and followed up with their supervisor to develop a plan to help that employee progress upward in their career. That is one important aspect of the notice characteristic of servant leadership. Helping someone else progress in their career brings tremendous joy.

The apostle Paul tells us to look out for the personal interests of others in Philippians 2:4. God is telling us to be aware of and to take notice of others so we can help diffuse the tension, fear, conflict, and stress in their lives and provide them encouragement and hope.

Taking notice also means you should become aware of when the people around you are struggling or hurting, and you can let God work through you to help support them and know when they need encouragement or prayer. As an employee, whom would you rather work with, a leader who wants to use you for their purposes and who doesn't have a clue about what you are going through, or a leader who cares about you and knows you well enough to know when you are struggling or suffering, and is there to support you?

I will never forget one night when I was leaving the corporate office late after a long day. A female colleague was helping me finalize a PowerPoint presentation I was going to make the following day. As I was leaving the office, I noticed the light was still on in her office. When I stuck my head in her office to see why she was working so late, she told me she was still working on revising the slides for the presentation I was to make the next day. I asked her to give me half of the deck so I could help her finish. I then went back in my office to work on the presentation, and, with both of us working on it, we were able to get the presentation finalized within a couple of hours.

I didn't think that much about it, but she told me she had never seen a senior executive do that type of work before. I told her it wasn't fair for her to have to work all night on my presentation, and I was more than happy to help out so she could get home to her family. After all, it was for *my* presentation! I heard about that incident over and over again as I traveled throughout the company. Little things like noticing when other members of your team are struggling and lending a hand resonates with employees and has a way of getting around the company and building trust.

Noticing as Discipleship

I have seen where developing my own sense of awareness of others and taking notice of others can lead to discipleship opportunities. Jesus commanded us as Christians to "go and make disciples" (Matthew 28:19). All of us have heard that before, but the Scripture says something different from what most people think. What it really says is we are to make disciples *as we are going*, which for us as business people can mean that as we are working, we should be making disciples of others.

As Christians, we are to be making disciples as we are doing whatever we are doing—as we are going. I have found getting to know the people I work with on a personal basis, and being more intentional about engaging with them on a personal basis and taking notice of them, has led to many discipling opportunities.

On many occasions throughout my career, just by noticing a person's demeanor was not what I typically encountered and then asking them about it led to further discussions about faith. For example, I remember an administrative support person that worked in one of our departments at the corporate office whom I got to know from being in the same office (she did not report directly to me).

One day I noticed that she appeared to be sad. When I asked her about it, she shared with me that her brother was in critical condition in the hospital. We talked about her brother, and I asked her if I could pray for him with her. That surprised her (I guess because we were in a work setting), and she said she would appreciate that very much. We prayed together, and then I told her I would keep her and her brother in my prayers.

During the following weeks I continued to stop by and ask about her brother when I was in the office and not away on business travel. One day she asked me if I would tell her more about my faith. She said she knew there was something different about me that gave me peace, and she asked me if I would be comfortable sharing that with her. I told her about my faith and shared the gospel with her. She asked me to help her pray a simple prayer to place her faith in Jesus Christ as her Lord and Savior.

That is just one example of many I could share with you, not to draw attention or glory to myself but to help you become more aware of the many opportunities we all have to do this in our workplaces. I hate to think of how many of those opportunities to take notice of someone that might have led to sharing the gospel that I let slip by during my career because I was either too focused on myself or just felt too busy to take notice at the time.

Noticing Yourself

Taking notice also means developing your own self-awareness. It means being aware how you come across to your colleagues. It means being aware of how they see you and learning when you need to switch gears. When you are under stress, sometimes your worst characteristics will become more evident to those around you. Developing the ability to take notice of yourself when you are under stress and becoming more self-aware of how you may be coming across to people is of vital importance. How do you want people to see you? How do you want people to think of you? How do you want people to remember you?

I always tried to have someone on my team I could trust and encourage to tell me how I was coming across to the rest of the team. After a meeting I would ask what they thought others heard me say. I wasn't doing this for gossip purposes. I did this so I could better understand how I was being perceived by others. I encouraged this person to tell me honestly and to give me the unvarnished truth so I could make adjustments or clarify things to others or the rest of the team.

It takes courage to want to hear the truth as a leader, and it takes courage for someone to speak honestly and boldly to help the leader improve. You have to make clear you want the truth so you can improve and so you can continue to build your relationships with other members of the team. For purposes of this discussion, I will call this trusted, courageous, unvarnished truth teller "Randy."

I recall one occasion when I asked Randy to share with me his observations about the meeting that just concluded and to describe how I came across to the team. He pointed out that he thought I may have hurt one of our colleague's feelings by not drawing them more into the discussion. At first, I was shocked by his comment and had to restrain myself from becoming defensive at his remark. (If I had become defensive, Randy would probably have become hesitant to give me the unvarnished truth in the future.)

We had just concluded a senior leadership team meeting where we had what I thought were some open and honest discussions about the strategic plan we were developing for the upcoming year. Most of the team had spoken up with their suggestions, ideas, and concerns. I left the meeting believing in my own mind that everyone had voiced their ideas and opinions and that we ended up with an approach everyone had bought into by the end of the meeting.

Randy pointed out there was one person in the meeting I failed to draw into the discussions more fully (I will call them the Quiet Colleague). The Quiet Colleague was one who had a difficult time speaking up to voice their concerns. This Quiet Colleague usually liked to think things through more thoroughly before voicing their opinion, particularly when a number of other more vocal people were expressing an opposing view to theirs.

It was certainly not my intention to steamroll the Quiet Colleague, and I quickly realized I had not done an adequate job of drawing them into our discussions so they would be comfortable expressing their own point of view. I had not facilitated the meeting in an effective way to give them a voice so their concerns could be considered as part of the mix in our discussions.

As I thought about what Randy was telling me, I knew he was right. I regretted that I may have inadvertently hurt the feelings of the Quiet Colleague, whom I knew from past experience, when they did speak up, usually brought something valuable to the team's attention that had not yet been considered and needed to be addressed.

I ended up gathering everyone back together for a follow-up meeting, to tell them I thought of some additional things we needed to consider and discuss. I did not say to everyone I was calling the meeting for purposes of allowing the Quiet Colleague to voice their concerns. That would have just embarrassed the Quiet Colleague.

In that subsequent meeting I was more intentional about drawing the Quiet Colleague into the discussion. The Quiet Colleague pointed out some things we had not considered previously, and quite frankly, had their points *not* been addressed prior to implementing the new strategic plan, we would have had some major problems. We ended up with a much better strategic plan than what we arrived at in the prior meeting and avoided what could have been a disaster.

Randy's coaching really helped me. In all future meetings I was much more intentional about drawing out the input from the Quiet Colleague. Sometimes I would even tell the Quiet Colleague in the middle of the meeting I wanted to hear what they had to say because they always had something valuable for us to consider, and I was going to come back to them in just a few minutes. That gave the Quiet Colleague time to think through what they wanted to say, and they were then much more comfortable voicing their point of view and participating in the discussions.

I found having someone on my team who would tell me honestly when I needed to make adjustments I failed to see myself, and then actually making those adjustments led to building tremendous trust from our team.

The Bible provides many examples where leaders relied on the prophets to speak boldly to them for guidance and for correction, rather than relying solely on themselves.

In 1 Kings 21, we see how the evil King of Israel, Ahab, listened to and took notice of the wise counsel given by the prophet Elijah. King Ahab wanted the vineyard next to his palace that was owned by Naboth so King Ahab could use it as a vegetable garden. When Naboth refused to sell King Ahab his vineyard, King Ahab became upset and quit eating. King Ahab's wife arranged to have Naboth killed so King Ahab could obtain Naboth's vineyard.

The Lord then told Elijah the prophet to tell King Ahab he and his wife provoked the Lord with their evil, and the Lord was going to bring evil to King Ahab's family. When Elijah confronted King Ahab, the king took notice of what Elijah was telling him. The king humbled himself before the Lord, and the Lord did not bring evil to King Ahab's family while King Ahab was alive. So even the evil king Ahab took counsel from Elijah to try to correct his evil ways. We also see in the Bible many accounts of Elisha, the successor to the prophet Elijah, advising various kings of Israel (2 Kings 6:8–23; 2 Kings 13:14–19).

King David took notice of the wise counsel of Nathan the prophet. One example of this is when King David wanted to build a house for the Lord. Nathan told King David the Lord did not want King David to build him a house (that would be done by David's son Solomon), but the Lord would establish His kingdom through David forever (2 Samuel 7). David followed Nathan's counsel and left it to his son Solomon to build the temple in Jerusalem.

Another example is when King David committed adultery with Bathsheba and arranged to have her husband stationed in a position during a battle that led to her husband's death so King David could hide Bathsheba's pregnancy. When Nathan confronted King David about his sin, King David acknowledged his sin to Nathan, which brought about King David's repentance and restoration with God (2 Samuel 12).

While I don't want to take these examples too far—as Elijah, Elisha, and Nathan were all prophets the Lord spoke through—I do think it illustrates how even the kings of Israel of the Old Testament did not rely solely on their own knowledge and trust in themselves but rather sought and took notice of the wise counsel from other godly people to help them correct their ways. We do well to do likewise by having others on our team and in our lives that can speak boldly to us, pray for us, hold us accountable, and provide us wise counsel and correction.

I previously discussed the importance of having mentors in chapter 6 on accountability. The point I want to emphasize here is the importance of reaching out to others who can help us notice how we are coming across to others or where we need to correct our ways. We can then make the needed adjustments we would not be aware of when we only trust in ourselves.

Let Others Notice You

Another aspect of notice is allowing your teammates to observe you on a deeper level than just a superficial relationship typically seen in the top-down leadership model. You can do this by making yourself vulnerable to others. While I discussed vulnerability in chapter 5 on empathy, the aspect of vulnerability I am talking about here involves sharing your own life struggles with others. This shows your colleagues that you, as the leader, don't view yourself as being any different from them, and you have the same struggles they have. This helps them connect with you as they begin to notice you are authentic and can be trusted.

As your own vulnerability allows others to notice you, you make it safe for them to show their own vulnerability and open up to you. Then you can notice more about them. That is where the power of notice can make a huge difference in your relationship. They see your vulnerability and that you are truly listening and caring; they in turn begin to do the same with you.

A tool I have used for decades to help bring a team together quickly by putting notice on steroids is a tool I call the Lifeline Exercise. I like to use this tool for team building, particularly when I put together an entirely new team or I place a new leader in an existing team.

In the Lifeline Exercise, I ask each person to plot on a piece of paper the major ups and downs of their life, beginning with their childhood to the present, and then connect the dots with a line. These ups and downs should be the major events in their life that were their highest points in their life (like getting a huge promotion, getting married, having a child, etc.) and their lowest points in their life (like getting divorced, getting fired, losing a child or another loved one). Keep in mind not everyone will be comfortable enough to share the details about each of these events with the other members of their team, and you should not force them to do so.

I always go first to discuss my lifeline to set the stage and allow people to see the major events that shaped who I am, like the challenges my wife and I have with our disabled daughter. Sharing my own struggles and showing my own vulnerability have always had the impact of drawing me closer to the people I share my story with. They in turn feel more comfortable opening up and showing their own vulnerability. I then ask others to share all or parts of their own lifeline story, to the extent they feel comfortable.

I have found that the Lifeline Exercise does more to bring a team together quickly than anything else I am aware of, as people begin to notice each other differently. People begin to see everyone has their own struggles, and some even share the same struggles. People learn things about one another that often take years to learn. It helps to show others how you get your unique perspective from the events that have shaped your life. It builds connections and trust within the team, and the more vulnerable people make themselves in sharing their own stories, the closer the connection and bond with others will become at the end of the exercise.

I have used the Lifeline Exercise for over twenty-five years with tremendous results every time I have used it. I have even used it with engaged couples I am counseling and in marriage enrichment classes with spouses who have been married for decades. Try it with your spouse. You might be surprised at what you learn about each other through the process!

This exercise should not be done quickly. I always give people at least thirty to forty-five minutes to build their lifeline, and then we take as much time as needed to share our lifeline stories with other members on the team. What everyone gets out of the exercise will be well worth the time invested.

The Lifeline Exercise also helps illustrate that none of us wants to be the cause of someone else's low point on their lifeline! Instead, we should all be trying to help others have a new high point to place on their lifeline.

The No-Stats All-Star

A professional athlete I believe demonstrates the notice aspects of servant leadership is Shane Battier. He was the 2001 Player of the Year with Duke University, winners of the NCAA National Championships that same year. Battier also played in the NBA with the Memphis Grizzlies, the Houston Rockets, and the Miami Heat (wining the National Championships in 2012 and 2013).

Battier is sometimes called the "No-Stats All-Star," a name that stuck with him after an article written by Michael Lewis (author of *Liar's Poker*, *The Big Short*, and *Moneyball*). Lewis pointed out that Battier didn't have the greatest personal statistics, but his team always scored more points when he was in the game compared to when he was not in the game. This statistic is called the "+/- stat" to indicate what impact a player has on his team's scoring just by being in the game.

Battier led in the stat of least amount of time in possession of the ball—passing the ball off to others quickly. He has said 98 percent of time he was on the court he didn't touch the ball, but he did things to support the team: boxing out, taking charges, running back on defense, or taking corner three-point shots.

Battier has said he would have rather taken more shots, but instead he chose to support his teammates by taking defenders away from the better shooters to allow them to make their shots. He said it is counterintuitive as a leader, but he always focused on what was within his control to contribute to his team by excelling at the little things.[2] Battier reminds me of how my dad always told me that my job as a leader was to remove the obstacles that got in the way of success and prevented others from excelling.

Battier said what he focused on as a leader was to "make it safe for the team to make mistakes . . . be authentic, provide support, and not criticism, and . . . what got you here won't get you to the next level."[3] Battier lived his servant leadership by being aware of and taking notice of others. He said, "The only thing I cared about was the success of my team. . . . Champions are made when no one is looking."[4]

Battier demonstrated how it is more important for the team to win than for him to get credit or take all the shots. Battier said, "Leadership has everything to do with how hard you work, not how much talent you have."[5] Bat-

---

2. *Shane Battier, The Art of the Intangible*, YouTube video, https://www.youtube.com/watch?v=wOgNqSi17oQ. Accessed September 7, 2020.

3. *Keynote Conference: An Interview with Shane Battier*, https://www.youtube.com/watch?v=Lt6xGGwC_4g. Accessed September 7, 2020.

4. *Shane Battier, The Art of the Intangible*, YouTube video, https//www.youtube.com/watch?v=wOgNqSi17oQ. Accessed September 7, 2020.

5. *Shane Battier: Leadership through Work Ethic,* https://www.youtube.com/watch?v=hY6tdhzDzBk. Accessed September 7, 2020.

tier showed his leadership by being aware of his teammates and by being aware of what he could do to help others succeed. As Battier demonstrated throughout his career, taking notice of and giving credit to others, and showing genuine appreciation for your teammates are key aspects of servant leadership.

Battier's taking notice of others can also be applied in the business setting by giving credit to others and showing appreciation to others. We recognized our employees in several ways for their meaningful contributions. We recognized them in our employee newsletter and not only mentioned their accomplishments but also let them tell a bit about their personal story. At the end of each year, we also gave awards to our employees who made significant contributions to the company's success or helped others in an exemplary manner.

Take the Blame, Not the Credit

Another important aspect of taking notice as a leader is to be the first to take the blame when something goes wrong and to be the first to give credit to others when things go right. In our customer-focused business at Waste Management, I valued the ability to make quick decisions based on the best available information and input from others, and I empowered others to do the same. It was important for me and people in the field to respond quickly to customer issues so we could show the customers we really cared.

The organizational model we developed for Waste Management was structured around the local market areas to empower decisions to be made locally rather than at the region or higher level in the organization, so we could respond to customers quickly.

I also valued that we were quick to determine if I or others made the wrong decision based on what we knew at the time. People on our team knew we were going to make the best decision we could based on everyone's input, and if it turned out later we made the wrong decision, I would be the first to say I made a mistake, and then we were quick to make the course correction.

The leader may not always be the one who directly caused something to go wrong, but when you empower others to make decisions, mistakes will be made and things will sometimes go wrong. If you blame others when things go wrong (and at times things *can* go wrong, and decisions can have unintended consequences), you can be assured your team will never step out and try things on their own ever again.

If you step up as the team leader and say you made the wrong decision and we now need to make some adjustments, you will endear your team to you unlike ever before by showing them you have their back. They will see you aren't just looking for someone else to blame and use to help propel you up in your own career. They will see by your actions that we are all in this to win together as a team.

I always told people we should expect mistakes but the key to success was identifying and correcting mistakes quickly and communicating those mistakes so we did not make the same mistake again. The key to being successful is to not make a mistake that could have been avoided by:

1. not noticing or considering other points of view that could provide wise counsel;
2. ignoring the facts; or
3. not learning from prior mistakes and, in any event, recovering quickly from the mistake.

"Whoever remains stiff-necked after many rebukes will suddenly be destroyed—without remedy" (Proverbs 29:1). If you don't seek out and take notice of wise counsel or to what others may be telling you to help you, you are headed down a path of ruin. When you make a mistake, you can't withdraw or try to hide the mistake, or you will destroy trust. You have to take responsibility for the mistake, acknowledge it, and own it. Apologize to the people who are impacted by your mistake, and recover strong.

And finally, when you have successes along the way, give credit to and notice other team members rather than taking credit yourself. Giving the credit to others will solidify the trust and respect they have for you as their leader. Being aware of how your words and actions impact others is of vital importance as you strive to take notice as a servant leader.

*"For we brought nothing into the world,
and we can take nothing out of it."*
1 TIMOTHY 6:7

CHAPTER 8

Recycling: One Man's Trash Is Another Man's Treasure

Joy and Contentment Are Infectious

IN THIS chapter we will discuss what it means to have joy and contentment as a servant leader. I am not talking about relying on the power of positive thinking as you live out your life like *The Little Engine That Could* ("I think I can, I think I can"), or the many programs in books and on television about the power of positive thinking. I am talking about the power that comes from being content with what God has already given you.

Contentment at Work

When I think about people I know who are so content with Jesus in their life they reflect the joy and love of Jesus in a way that actually infects those around them with their joy, one of those people that always comes to my mind is the Port-O-Let driver (his name is Fred) I worked with in the *Undercover Boss* show. I never met Fred before being assigned to him as my boss for the day on the Waste Management

Undercover Boss episode, and I worked with him undercover as his helper cleaning out Port-O-Lets all day.

I have to be honest with you, when I heard I was going to have a job cleaning out Port-O-Lets all day, I thought it was going to be a long day I would not enjoy very much. I knew it would be a tough, stinky job! But honestly, that day was one of the most fun days I had of all the different jobs I did for the *Undercover Boss* show. And the reason I had so much fun was because of Fred's positive and fun attitude. He showed how a happy disposition, when you are filled with the love of Jesus Christ, can make even a stinky job fun for you and everyone around you.

I have never laughed so much while doing work. In fact, after eight hours of working with him that day, my face muscles were fatigued from laughing so much that I kept getting cramps in my face. I have never had that happen to me before! He and I were having so much fun laughing with each other, we had a crowd around us at the Houston Live Stock Show and Rodeo where that part of the episode was being filmed, because the crowd thought we were some kind of comedy act!

While it didn't make the *Undercover Boss* show (I guess it was edited out), at one point I asked Fred if he was a Christian because I could just tell there was something inside of him giving him all that joy. Fred told me he was a Christian, and he guessed I was too! We hugged each other, said a prayer together, and then just kept on working. Jesus Christ was clearly evident in his life.

Fred taught me how important it is to let that joy and contentment with what you have shine on those around you and what an impact that can have on others. It is so infectious and draws others to you because they want to know the reason for the hope that is within you.

Several verses come to my mind when I think of my time working with Fred on the Port-O-Let truck:

- "Gracious words are a honeycomb, sweet to the soul and healing to the bones" (Proverbs 16:24).
- "A cheerful heart is good medicine, but a crushed spirit dries up the bones" (Proverbs 17:22).

I will never forget the joyful heart of contentment I experienced working with Fred on the Port-O-Let truck that day! And I am delighted we continue our friendship even today.

Contentment in Our Culture

The Bible has a lot to say about being content. I hope to show you that filling your life with Jesus Christ will bring contentment. I hope you will see God wants us to be content. He loves us dearly and wants the best for us.

Our culture tries to tell us that pursuing everything other than God will bring us contentment. People are searching hopelessly for contentment by pursuing material things or their own selfish desires and pleasures, but they aren't seeking God. With all the material things we have compared to what the rest of the world has, why are so many people unhappy and so unfulfilled?

We can see it all around us at work—people pouring their lives into their work with a focus on themselves, getting ahead, and making a name for themselves. I am sure everyone can identify someone they know (or maybe even you are that person) that on the outside seems to have achieved much in their career—their position, their status, their home or homes, their car or cars, etc. Yet, even with all the material possessions they have, deep down the people who have not placed their faith in Jesus Christ are not happy. They are not content. But they just keep pursuing more and more of the same stuff.

I think that is why there is such a huge drug and alcohol problem in the world. People are trying to find contentment with drugs, alcohol, pornography, and material things because they think those things will bring them contentment or comfort or take away their pain. Those things might provide a brief relief from some of life's pains and struggles, but they will never find lasting contentment and peace without Jesus in their life and turning control over to God.

Advertising is a huge business because marketing teams can convince people through ads that if they just buy this one thing, they will be filled with joy and contentment. People who try to fill their life with drugs, alcohol, pornography, and material things will never be happy without God. The Bible tells us in Genesis 1:26 that God made us in His image. God loves us and He wants a relationship with us. Without God we won't be happy.

Contentment in Adversity

Most of the Scripture about contentment in the New Testament is written by the apostle Paul. Many of you know about Paul's background, but some of you may not. Paul was a Jewish leader who looked for Christians to arrest and bring in for persecution. You might say he hated Christians and terrorized them. But then Jesus appeared to Paul after Jesus had been crucified, died, buried, and rose from the dead. Paul then placed his faith in Jesus Christ as his Lord and Savior and began his ministry of preaching the gospel and starting new churches. Paul ended up writing about half of the New Testament.

Paul was arrested for teaching that Jesus Christ died for our sins and rose again and that by placing your faith in Him, you can have your sins forgiven and be assured of eternal life with Jesus Christ in heaven when you die. Paul was beaten, placed in chains, tortured, and eventually died a martyr's death because of his faith in Jesus Christ, but Paul never did anything to deserve that punishment. So if anyone should have had an attitude that life is not fair and be discontent, it is Paul. But Paul placed his faith in Jesus Christ.

Paul was content, no matter what His situation, because Paul trusted God. Let's look at what Paul teaches us about contentment.

> But godliness with contentment is great gain.
> For we brought nothing into the world, and we
> can take nothing out of it. But if we have food
> and clothing, we will be content with that. Those
> who want to get rich fall into temptation and a
> trap and into many foolish and harmful desires
> that plunge people into ruin and destruction.
> For the love of money is a root of all kinds of evil.

Some people, eager for money, have wandered from the faith and pierced themselves with many griefs.

But you, man of God, flee from all this, and pursue righteousness, godliness, faith, love, endurance and gentleness. Fight the good fight of the faith. Take hold of the eternal life to which you were called when you made your good confession in the presence of many witnesses. (1 Timothy 6:6–12)

Paul says we can't take anything with us when we die. Every time I read that verse I am reminded of a George Strait song (a famous country singer from Texas) who reminds us in his song "You'll Be There," that you'll never see a hearse with a luggage rack. You can't take it with you.

I think Paul is saying that living the life Christ intends for us does not have going after money and material possessions as its primary goal. That doesn't mean we shouldn't work to provide for our family or save money. And the Bible doesn't say that people who have money are evil. God may have blessed them with money because they are good stewards of God's money rather than worshiping their money and believing it is their money.

I believe Paul is telling us if our primary goal in life is to pursue and love money and material possessions, we are not going to be content. Paul says the *love of money* (not money in and of itself) will lead to ruin and destruction and will bring grief.

Paul, while he is in chains in prison, tells us: "I am not saying this because I am in need, for I have learned to be content whatever the circumstances. I know what it is to be in need, and I know what it is to have plenty. I have learned the secret of being content in any and every situation, whether well fed or hungry, whether living in plenty or in want. I can do all this through him who gives me strength" (Philippians 4:11–13).

The last sentence of this verse is usually taken out of context when people quote it. It is really talking about contentment. It is about knowing God will give us what we need. God is always with us as Christians (Matthew 28:20). As discussed in chapter 6 on accountability, being content and trusting God through our trials can even reflect God to others.

Remember, the apostle Paul was in chains in a Roman prison when he wrote this letter to the Philippians. Paul had done no wrong and was arrested because he was preaching the gospel of Jesus Christ. Paul knew he was doing the will of God. And he knew it was part of God's plan for him to be in prison. He didn't cry out to God and ask why he was in chains in prison or whine and say, "This is not fair."

In fact Paul tells us in Philippians 1:14 that because he was chained to Roman guards so he couldn't escape, he even used that opportunity to tell the guards about Jesus. The Bible tells us that many Roman guards even placed their faith in Jesus Christ as their Lord and Savior because of Paul's testimony to them. Can you imagine being one of those Roman guards and being chained to Paul preaching to you all day?

So Paul was content, even though he was wrongfully placed in chains in prison.

We can learn a lot from Paul. Paul focused on living his life every day to serve the Lord. Paul was content no matter what his circumstances because he trusted the Lord. Paul did not find his contentment in his material possessions or his job status. Paul found his contentment by knowing he belonged to Jesus Christ and from the peace he possessed knowing he was doing God's will while on this earth and that he would have eternal life with Jesus.

Paul says he can do anything through Jesus Christ who gives him strength. Paul didn't draw his strength from having more material possessions than his friends or from worrying about what others thought about him. Paul's contentment did not come from the material things of the world, or from money or status. Paul's faith in Jesus Christ brought him contentment. Paul got his strength from God. Paul says he can do all things through the strength he gets from Jesus Christ.

Discontentment

The opposite of contentment is discontentment. Discontentment is to be unhappy, whining, grumbling, complaining all the time, thinking life is not fair, wanting things you don't have, being envious of what others have, and not being thankful for what God has given to you. Do you know anyone like that? Are you ever like that? I think we all are like that every now and then.

In 1 Timothy 6:6–12, quoted above, we see what discontentment is: discontentment is ungodly. It is wanting to be rich with money and material things to bring ourselves glory. It is wanting more than you need. It is a trap that can ruin us and destroy us. And it is the love of money and material things.

Discontentment can lead you away from God. Discontentment shows that we really don't trust God. It shows we are weak in our faith, and we have not submitted to God to allow Him to run our lives. The Bible has lots of stories about people who were discontent with what God gave them and how discontentment led to their ruin.

Just take a look at the first story in the Bible about Adam and Eve in Genesis 3 (the first book in the Bible). Adam and Eve were tempted by Satan so that they wanted more than what God gave to them. God gave them everything God created in the garden except God told them they were not to eat of the fruit of one tree.

The garden was a perfect place for Adam and Eve to live. But they were tempted by Satan and were not content with what God gave them. They rebelled and wanted to be like God, so they ate fruit from the one tree God had forbidden them to eat from. And it led to all of our ruin. Their discontentment led them to sin. Their discontentment led to their being kicked out of the garden and separated from God. So, do you see how discontentment with what God has given to us can lead to sin and separation from God?

The Source for Contentment

Unfortunately, our sinful nature, along with Satan, are at work every day to try to convince us we are not content. Paul tells us what we must do to overcome our discontentment in 1 Timothy 6:11, quoted above. He tells us we will find contentment by pursuing righteousness, godliness, faith, love, endurance, and gentleness. Paul is telling us to focus on our relationship with God, and that will bring us contentment.

Paul goes on to tell us this is not easy, that it is going to be a fight and a struggle (1 Timothy 6:12). It is a battle, but it is a battle worth fighting. If we focus on pursuing godliness, faith, love, endurance, and gentleness, we can overcome discontentment and find contentment in our growing relationship with Jesus Christ.

So contentment is a spiritual issue, not a money issue or an issue about how many material possessions we have. I think the secret to contentment is understanding God is sovereign and in control. If God doesn't want something to happen, it won't happen. That means God is in control when good things happen in our lives, and God is in control when times are tough for us.

Contentment does not mean things always go our way or that we are always comfortable. As I have mentioned throughout this book, I became angry at God when the doctor made the mistake that led to my daughter's lifetime of suffering, brain damage, and physical disabilities. While I didn't lose my faith, I couldn't understand how God could let this happen to such a precious two-month-old little girl who had no capacity to sin. It just didn't seem fair! I was anything but content!

But God helped me understand that as long as my focus was in the wrong place, I was not going to find contentment. I was focused on my own plan and how this tragedy with Linley was going to keep her from doing all the things I wanted to do with her. I felt cheated. Contentment was not even a possibility for me as long as I focused on myself.

Once the Holy Spirit opened my eyes to see that God had a different plan for my daughter—a plan that would bring God glory—and that I needed to trust God and be content with His plan, I found peace and contentment. I couldn't have found contentment without trusting God first.

Contentment is not based on what is going on outside of our bodies, and it is not based on the material things we have. Contentment is based on what is in our heart. Contentment is only found in God. Lasting contentment can only come when we rely on Jesus Christ for everything and turn control over to Him. As Paul tells us, we can do all things through Jesus Christ who gives us strength (Philippians 4:13).

So the secret to contentment is our relationship with Jesus Christ. None of us will be content without Jesus Christ in our life. Our nature is to sin, complain, and want more than God has given to us. If all we keep pursuing is momentary happiness and pleasure through material things, there is no way we will ever be content. If we don't have Jesus Christ, we won't have the ability to be content in this life. We will be trying to fill our life with momentary pleasures rather than filling our life with Him.

If we are not 100 percent certain that when our short journey here on this earth is over we will be in heaven with Jesus Christ for eternity, then we will never be content in this life. (And if you are not 100 percent certain that you will go to heaven when you die, please stay with me through the end of the book).

We all know many people who are unhappy with their spouse. Maybe that is even you. Many leave one spouse thinking the next spouse is going to solve their problem, only to find they now have twice as many problems. The problem is not their spouse. Their problem is their selfishness and trying to fill their life by pursuing their selfish desires for momentary pleasures rather than focusing on Jesus Christ and letting Him CLEAN up their life and help them live the way God intended us to live. Remember what Paul told us in 1 Timothy 6:11—contentment comes by focusing on "righteousness, godliness, faith, love, endurance and gentleness."

Now I am not telling you that just because we place our faith in Jesus Christ we are going to have instant contentment for the rest of our lives. I wish that were true! Remember, Paul told us life would be a battle. We must focus on Jesus Christ by reading the Bible, praying, and asking the Holy Spirit to help us develop godliness, faith, love, endurance, and gentleness. By putting our faith in Jesus Christ, turning control of our lives over to Him, and allowing the Holy Spirit to work in our lives as the Holy Spirit indwells us as believers—as we read in Philippians 4:13—we will be able to do all things through Jesus Christ who strengthens us.

Contentment comes to us when we depend on God rather than ourselves. Contentment can come to us when we give to others in need, not just of our money but of our time to help them as servant leaders. One of the things God has taught me that has helped me greatly with my own contentment is that neither my money *nor my time* is mine. My money *and my time* are both given to me by God. No matter how much or how little each of us has, it is still more than we deserve because God owes us nothing. Everything we possess is a gift from God. And God wants us to be a good steward of everything He has given to us.

The apostle Peter tells us, "Each of you should use whatever gift you have received to serve others, as faithful stewards of God's grace in its various forms" (1 Peter 4:10). God wants all of us to spend the money and the time He has given us wisely and in a way that brings glory to God. And when I am doing that, I have contentment.

Contentment does not mean getting what you want; it means being happy with what God has given you. Contentment is being thankful for what you have instead of constantly thinking about what you don't have. I have found that the more of my time I give away to help others as a servant leader, the more content I am!

That is one of the reasons I am devoting the time to write this book, with the profits from sales going to charity. The hope that some of you reading this book might be helped in some way and the thought of the profits from the sale of this book helping people in need bring me great joy and contentment. And hopefully it will bring glory to God, not me.

Another thing I have found that contributes greatly to contentment is telling God how thankful I am for all He has given me—even thanking Him for the little things He does in my life every single day. The more I thank God, the more I become aware of what He has done for me and the more contentment I find myself. The apostle Paul tells us: "Rejoice always, pray continually, give thanks in all circumstances; for this is God's will for you in Christ Jesus" (1 Thessalonians 5:16–18).

As discussed in chapter 6 on accountability, we can even find contentment in difficult times. Maybe God is trying to teach us something through our crises. We can give thanks to God even when times are tough that He is taking an interest in us to teach us something and to draw us closer in our relationship to Him. Paul tells us, "What, then, shall we say in response to these things? If God is for us, who can be against us? He who did not spare his own Son, but gave him up for us all—how will he not also, along with him, graciously give us all things" (Romans 8:31–32).

So I ask you now, how much contentment do you have? How often do you rejoice and thank God for what He has provided for you? Or do you spend more time thinking: *What if this, or what if that? If only this would happen, my life would be great.* I fall in that same trap. I begin to think about Linley: *What if the medical accident had not happened to her? What would she have done in high school—would she have been a cheerleader or an athlete? What would she have studied in college? What job would she have now? What would it have been like to walk her down the aisle to get married? Would she be giving us grandchildren now? What if, what if?* Then I realize again that I am not being content with what God has given me. Linley has brought tremendous joy to our lives.

Through many answered prayers Linley continues to inspire me through her challenging life. Even with her many mental and physical disabilities, surgeries, stays in intensive care on average of about every four years of her life, Linley has made more of a positive impact on peoples' lives than I ever will. What tremendous glory Linley has brought to God through her inspiration to so many people! Through all her daily pain and challenges, she never complains about her pain. She is my inspiration every day!

I think we all have work to do when it comes to contentment. Next time you find yourself feeling down or that life is unfair, just remember Paul being wrongfully chained in a Roman prison, and yet he was joyous and content. I doubt any of our lives will be as difficult as Paul's was in prison. But we can be just as content by placing our focus on Jesus Christ, being thankful for all God has given us, and asking the Holy Spirit to help us grow in our ability to live with righteousness, godliness, faith, love, endurance, and gentleness. Ultimately, our contentment comes as a result of our faith in Jesus Christ as our Lord and Savior.

"If it is possible, as far as it depends on you, live at peace with everyone. . . . Do not be overcome by evil, but overcome evil with good."

ROMANS 12:18, 21

CHAPTER 9

Taking Out the Trash

What Do You Need to Turn over to God?

WARNING: I encourage you to read this chapter when you have some time to think about your own leadership style, any relationships that are not where they should be, and your current relationship with God. This will be a difficult chapter for many readers to process because you will need to be honest with yourself and do some self-reflection to get the most out of this chapter. If you don't think you are in the mood for that right now, I encourage you to skip this chapter and then come back to it when you think you are ready.

I WILL begin by asking you an important question. I want you to read it, and then I want you to stop and give it some serious thought: What are you hanging onto that is taking up space in your brain or your life and preventing you from trusting God with everything and turning control over to Him? Now think about that for a while and then write it down on a piece of paper. Return to this page after you have done that. Don't come back to this chapter until then.

I once heard Richard Ellis, a dear friend and spiritual mentor who is a pastor in Dallas (www.richardellistalks. com), say if you have more treasure stored up here in this life than you have stored up in heaven, you are in trouble. I think what Pastor Richard means is that we should constantly pursue God's will for our life so that what we are doing will bring glory to God. God does not want us to fill our lives with earthly possessions we can't take with us. We need to let go of those pursuits of material possessions on this earth and turn our lives over to God to pursue the life He wants us to live.

The apostle Matthew tells us: "No one can serve two masters. Either you will hate the one and love the other, or you will be devoted to the one and despise the other. You cannot serve both God and money" (Matthew 6:24). We are stewards of all God gives us, money and time. How are you being a steward of the money and time God has given you? Are you investing any of it in others? One of my biggest aha moments was when I came to realize God has given me all the time I have in my life. What am I doing with it? How am I using my time to bring God glory?

I used to get frustrated when I was inconvenienced with something that delayed me from my plans for the day. I was so proud about how efficient and productive I was. I always felt like I made the most of my time, and I seldom wasted any time. But man, just let an unexpected delay or inconvenience pop up, and I became frustrated because something or some-one was interfering with *my time*!

I must be honest with you, I have not perfected this yet, but I am much more aware that time is not *my time*; it is *God's time* that He has given to me. Now, when I am inconvenienced, or something unexpected comes up to take me off my plans for the day, I try to stop and think, *OK God, what are You doing here? What are You trying to teach me, or whom are You directing me to talk to? What is this all about? How will this inconvenience bring glory to You? What do You want me to do?*

As I have explained throughout this book, and maybe it is the same for you, I used to approach my life with the feeling of "I got this." Sure, I was a Christian, but I still thought my life was all about me and that I was in control of it. I thought with proper planning and hard work I could accomplish my goals and almost anything else I determined to do. As I discussed in chapter 1, it took the shipwreck with my daughter to teach me I am not in control. It is not about my plan. I need to focus on God's plan.

What things do you need to let go of and turn control over to God? What things do you need to first seek His will about? Where have you been charging ahead in full pursuit without asking God what He thinks about your plan? Think about what is working in your life and what is not working, and then ask God, "What do I need to start doing, and what do I need to stop doing?"

If you talk to God, He can help you: "If you accept my words and store up my commands within you, turning your ear to wisdom and applying your heart to understanding—indeed, if you call out for insight and cry aloud for understanding, and if you look for it as for silver and search for it as for hidden treasure, then you will understand the fear of the LORD and find the knowledge of God. For the LORD gives wisdom; from his mouth comes knowledge and understanding" (Proverbs 2:1–6).

You and I aren't the only ones who think, *We got this*, from time to time. The Bible has lots of stories about people who think the same way, and it turns out to be a disaster for them. But it takes the disaster for them to realize their error. Let's take a look at a few examples, which I will summarize below (however, I encourage you to read the entire stories in the Bible).

Joshua

The first example shows us what happens when we don't seek God's will for our lives. Joshua was taking the Israelites into the promised land after Mosses died. As the Israelites encountered people who were living in the promised land, Joshua would speak to the Lord to get instructions from the Lord on how to proceed in the upcoming battle to take the promised land from the inhabitants.

However, in Joshua 9, we read that the Israelites came upon some strangers in the promised land. The Israelites did not know whether these strangers were living in the promised land and were enemies of the Israelites who would fight to prevent them from coming into the promised land or if these people were just passing through the promised land from a different area and meant the Israelites no harm. Joshua and his men "did not ask for the counsel of the LORD" about these strangers (Joshua 9:14 NASB).

Instead, the Israelites asked the strangers where they were from. The strangers lied and said they were from a land far away (even though they really lived right there in the promised land). We read on to see that the Israelites made a peace agreement with these strangers. The Israelites swore an oath to God that they would not harm these strangers, but they made the peace agreement and oath without first seeking counsel from the Lord.

When the Israelites later learned the strangers lied to them, the Israelites were not able to do battle with these strangers because the Israelites swore an oath to God that they would not harm those strangers. This shows what can happen when we fail to seek counsel of the Lord. The Israelites thought, *I got this.* Always a mistake to try and go it alone without God!

King David

King David is a great example of someone who consistently sought God's will before he went into battle. "So David inquired of God again, and God answered him, 'Do not go directly after them, but circle around them and attack them in front of the poplar trees. As soon as you hear the sound of marching in the tops of the poplar trees, move out to battle, because that will mean God has gone out in front of you to strike the Philistine army.' So David did as God commanded him, and they struck down the Philistine army, all the way from Gibeon to Gezer" (1 Chronicles 14:14–16). (For other examples see 1 Samuel 23, 30; 2 Samuel 2, 5.)

These verses show us how important it is that we seek God's will always and trust that He is with us always. The

New Testament tells us how foolish it is to make plans without consulting God first, and thinking *I got this*: "Now listen, you who say, 'Today or tomorrow we will go to this or that city, spend a year there, carry on business and make money.' Why, you do not even know what will happen tomorrow. What is your life? You are a mist that appears for a little while and then vanishes. Instead, you ought to say, 'If it is the Lord's will, we will live and do this or that.' As it is, you boast in your arrogant schemes. All such boasting is evil" (James 4:13–16).

Don't get me wrong, making plans is not evil or wrong. In fact, planning is wise. But we should always pray to God as we are planning, seek His guidance, and be ready to make adjustments to our plans. We don't know what will happen tomorrow, but He knows everything past, present, and future. And we should always say, "If God is willing."

Forgiveness

Let me conclude this chapter by talking about one other possible bit of trash in your life you may need to turn over to God. This is about holding a grudge against others you think have wronged you in the past.

Are there people you don't get along with at work or in your family? Are there people you would love to get revenge against? If you keep hanging on to that trash, it will tear you up. It will consume your thoughts. And it will keep you from being a servant leader people want to follow. You need to let go of that trash and give it to God. Toss it! The apostle Paul tells us:

Do not repay anyone with evil for evil. Be careful to do what is right in the eyes of everyone. If it is possible, as far as it depends on you, live at peace with everyone. Do not take revenge, my dear friends, but leave room for God's wrath, for it is written: "It is mine to avenge; I will repay," says the Lord. On the contrary, "If your enemy is hungry, feed him; if he is thirsty, give him something to drink. In doing this, you will heap burning coals on his head." Do not be overcome by evil, but overcome evil with good. (Romans 12:17–21)

It took me a long time to come to the point I could forgive the doctor who caused all of Linley's pain and suffering. For a long time I was consumed with what I might be able to do to make sure that doctor never was in a position to injure someone else the way he injured my precious Linley. I just couldn't get out of my mind how mad I was at him for causing all of Linley's needless pain and suffering. All of that suffering could have been avoided if he just used the correct instrument on her during the test.

It took a long time for the Holy Spirit to work on my heart so I could realize the doctor did not come to work that day with the intention of ruining my daughter's life. He didn't wake up that morning thinking, *What precious little girl can I harm so badly today that she will have brain damage, a life of physical disabilities, challenges, pain and suffering, and take away all the joy her family can have with her?*

It took a while for me to realize he just made a mistake in choosing the wrong instrument. It was not an intentional mistake. He was trying to do his best to help our daughter. We all make mistakes every day.

The Holy Spirit made it possible for me to forgive that doctor. And when I threw away that trash in my life, my hatred for that doctor, and being consumed with how I could make him pay for what he did, a tremendous peace came over me. God gave me the strength to get that trash off my mind and out of my life and showed me the power of empathy and caring for others. It has totally changed my life.

Let Go of Your Trash

So now I want you to pick up that piece of paper I asked you to write on at the beginning of this chapter. Take a moment to read what you wrote down. Now wad up that piece of paper and throw it away. Yes, throw that trash into the garbage can right now! I hope you see from this chapter that you don't need to be hauling that trash around with you in your brain and in your life. It will consume you and will prevent you from living the fulfilled life God wants you to have.

Now think about it. What do you do with your household trash? You have to take your trash outside and possibly even to the street curb to get it hauled away. Trash collectors typically don't come inside your house to pick up your trash. I hope what you wrote on your piece of paper includes some of the personal trash you have in your own life you want to lay at the foot of the cross so it can be hauled away and be taken out of your life by God. Everyone needs to have great *management* in your own life, or you will end up *wasting* your life, wasting the opportunities God has given you, and choosing to be *management waste.*

I invite you right now to thank God for all He has already given you in your life. Be specific about what you are thankful for. And then tell God to take whatever you wrote on that paper and to give you the strength to depend on Him to remove it from your life. Tell God you want to turn your life over to Him, to give you the strength to trust Him with your life, and to show you His will for your life.

The prophet Isaiah tells us: "Wash and make yourselves clean. Take your evil deeds out of my sight; stop doing wrong" (Isaiah 1:16). Tell God you want Him to take that trash away and to help you begin to use the CLEAN principles in this book to CLEAN up your life so you can be the person He designed you to be rather than *management waste*! Then get ready to experience incredible joy as the Holy Spirit helps you focus on others rather than yourself. It is a game changer indeed!

*"I no longer call you servants,
because a servant does not know his master's
business. Instead, I have called you friends,
for everything that I learned from my Father
I have made known to you."*

JOHN 15:15

CHAPTER 10

Exit Strategy

When You Leave Your Job

WHEN I look back over my career, I found I was ready for a career change about every ten years. I practiced law in private practice for almost ten years. I worked at Baker Hughes for almost ten years. I worked at Waste Management for ten and half years. And I was with Rockwater (CEO, chairman of the board, followed by lead director after I stepped down as CEO) for about seven years (I stepped down early to help my wife care for our daughter when she developed a hole in her heart and we didn't think she would survive, although I am still a shareholder).

As I previously stated, I always tried to put people on my team who were smarter than I am and who possessed skills I didn't have. I believe the strength of a leader can be judged by the quality of the talent and people they surround themselves with.

I knew if I surrounded myself with people just like me, then we were not going to have a strong team. Sure, I brought certain things to the team, but the strength of the team was in the collective strength of the individual members of the team, not from what I brought to the team.

Optimal Team Design

Over the years of leading various teams, I have come to the conclusion a servant leader should have no more than nine to twelve direct reports. I think nine to ten direct reports is optimal, and beyond that you start getting stretched thin and can't develop the close relationships you need to be an effective servant leader.

Even Jesus, who is God, only chose twelve disciples to lead and teach. He also prayed to God the Father before He chose His team (Luke 6:12–13). I believe we should follow Jesus' example of servant leadership. Jesus thought about and prayed about each of the twelve people before He put them on His team. Jesus then trusted the men He put on His team and considered them friends, not servants.

Jesus also made sure His Disciples (His team, if you will) knew His business: "I no longer call you servants, because a servant does not know his master's business. Instead, I have called you friends, for everything that I learned from my Father I have made known to you" (John 15:15).

Jesus communicated to His team the things they needed to know. Jesus told His disciples, "The knowledge of the secrets of the kingdom of heaven has been given to you, but not to them" (Matthew 13:11).

Jesus wanted people on His team who would follow Him so He could teach them and model for them how He wanted them to live and operate, and then He sent them out to lead others in the same way. The apostle Mark tells us Jesus "appointed twelve that they might be with him and that he might send them out to preach" (Mark 3:14).

Jesus also picked people to be on his team who would stand by Him during tough times. Jesus told His disciples: "For who is greater, the one who is at the table or the one who serves? Is it not the one who is at the table? But I am among you as one who serves. You are those who have stood by me in my trials. And I confer on you a kingdom, just as my Father conferred one on me, so that you may eat and drink at my table in my kingdom and sit on thrones, judging the twelve tribes of Israel" (Luke 22:27–30).

Jesus had a purpose for each disciple he picked for His team. Peter would be the rock upon which the church would be built (Matthew 16:18). Jesus even had a reason to pick Judas, who would later betray Jesus, which was all part of God's plan for our salvation. Jesus told his disciples: "'Yet there are some of you who do not believe.' For Jesus had known from the beginning which of them did not believe and who would betray him" (John 6:64).

Jesus modeled servant leadership for us, from how He chose and built His team to how He was committed to and cared about His team, and to how He trained, developed, and commissioned His team to proceed with His mission of building His church after He ascended to the right hand of the Father. We can learn from Jesus' model of servant leadership in building and developing our team.

When Is It Time to Leave Your Job?

By surrounding myself with people who were good at what they brought to the team, at some point I am the one blocking them from continuing to move up in their career. I have just always felt after about ten years, it is time for me to move on, get out of the way, and allow other members of the team to move up and lead the team to even greater heights. I always missed the people on our team when I left, and I can tell you I actually shed tears on the day I left every company I worked for. But my leaving the team then allowed someone else to bring new energy to the team after I left and allowed me to start a new team and bring new energy to the new team.

I feel strongly that too many leaders stay in one place for far too long. This can lead to complacency and stagnation for the team and for the leaders themselves. It is too easy to sit back and get comfortable in a position you have been in for more than ten years. In fact, I personally don't believe any CEO should stay at the same company as CEO for more than ten years. I believe a new CEO will bring new ideas and energy to help lead the company to new heights, and the departing CEO will be able to serve a new company better with their renewed energy than continuing in the same place for decades.

I understand my approach of leaving a great job and a great team I cared about deeply every ten years may not be for everyone. I am certainly not telling you that you are wrong if you don't follow my model. I am merely providing you my thoughts to get you to think about your own journey.

The bottom line is you should pray for guidance from God, and then when He tells you it is time to move, you need to trust Him and be ready to move on. Think about how long you feel you can be effective in your current leadership role and when it may be time to move on to allow others an opportunity to lead and to provide yourself an opportunity to reenergize and bring new energy to a new team.

Leaving the Right Way

I always felt one of the most important responsibilities in my job as a leader was to train others who would be ready to lead the team following my eventual departure. That is exactly what Jesus did with His disciples. When He ascended to heaven, He left to the disciples whom He had trained the responsibility to carry on the mission He trained them to do—to spread the gospel and to make disciples makers to build the kingdom.

Seeing people on the teams I have been on continue to advance in their own careers long after I have been gone has given me great joy. I have been so happy to see the people I spent time mentoring and training go on to achieve great success in their own careers.

When it is time to move on, the best thing you can leave with is the respect of all your colleagues. To do well as a servant leader, you have to dedicate yourself to the CLEAN principles: being *committed* to each person on your team; *listening* to them by giving them a voice; *empowering* them to be their best; being *accountable* to them and showing them how to contribute to the team's success; and taking *notice* of them by showing appreciation for their contributions.

If you have done that, then you have created a team people love to be on and a team where people are fully energized and engaged. Then, when it is time for you to depart, you will have positioned yourself to be able to move on and turn the reins over to others who are prepared, and you will leave with the kind of respect from your team that will continue long after you leave. You will have made a positive difference in the lives of others that they will never forget.

I felt genuine love for the members of my team at every job I left. While I knew it was God's will for me to move on and I was excited about the new opportunity ahead for me, as well being thrilled about the new responsibilities some of the members of the team would soon have with my departure, I was also overcome with emotion as the day for my departure approached. I always spent the last days in each job I had going around thanking and shaking hands with every teammate because I knew I would never be that close to them again. I knew I would miss the daily interactions with them. And it always brought tears to my eyes.

Waste Management has so many employees that all I did for the last several weeks I was there was go around and thank every single employee at every level of the organization I could find. It was a moving experience for me. But the thanks many people expressed to me as I was leaving, and the phone calls and notes I continue to receive from folks even today, thanking me for the difference they feel I made in their lives (which was really God working through me to impact their lives) is tremendously meaningful and gratifying to me, and I can only give thanks to God for those blessings He has poured out on me.

I still communicate regularly with many employees across North America and even around the world that I worked with throughout my decades-long career. I have continued to try to stay in touch with many of my former colleagues. It is always fun to tell the same old stories all over again and share some laughs about the "good old days" before we forget those stories. I continue to help others by being available to discuss some of their challenges with them and to help them think through some of the alternatives, or to serve as a reference for them as they continue to move up in their careers. This, too, gives me tremendous joy.

Maintaining relationships is so important for a servant leader. Even as I moved to new jobs as I progressed in my own career, I found that maintaining relationships with people from my previous jobs was vital. It was exciting to tap into talent from the places I previously worked, to offer many people new opportunities of increased responsibility, to help them continue to move up in their own careers, and to bring their energy and skills to a new team. Even in my current semi-retirement from being a business executive, I am still helping others find new career opportunities. Seeing others continue to progress in their successful careers, and to see them having a positive impact on others as servant leaders, is personally rewarding to me.

The apostle Paul continued to write letters to the churches he helped establish (see the letters in the New Testament that Paul wrote to churches in various cities), thanking them and continuing to reach out to maintain his connection with them and to help them grow in their walk with the Lord. Paul also continued to pray for them. Paul shows that our lives as servant leaders are all about relationships with others and how important it is to maintain those connections even after we have moved on.

At the end of Paul's Letter to the Romans in the New Testament, he tells the believers in Rome to say hello to thirty-three fellow believers in Rome. At the time of his writing the Letter to the Romans, Paul had not yet visited Rome, yet he knew each of the people he mentioned on a personal basis and knew what they were doing in Rome (Romans 16:1–16). Paul didn't have a cell phone or the Internet to keep up with them! What a fantastic model Paul is for us in how we should develop personal relationships with the people we work with, pray for them, and keep up with them in their own careers long after we move on.

As we close out this chapter, let me go back to expand on a point I made in chapter 2 about bad bosses. As I have previously discussed, I learned a lot from some of the worst bosses I worked for. I learned I did not want to be that type of leader. I want to encourage you again if you are in that situation currently with a bad boss, hang in there. God may have you in a learning experience that will serve you well later in your career, just as He did with me.

As Christians, we must remember that we are not perfect either. We don't want to look at others and hope for justice so they will be punished in some way for their bad actions. Remember, God has forgiven us of all our sins and our failings. God also created all of us, even our bad bosses. Nobody is perfect, and we all have periods in our lives where we do not live as God wants us to live. We have all said things and acted in ways we wish we could take back. And yet God still loves us and has forgiven us.

God created that bad boss, and He loves them too. Maybe God wants to work through you to help change that bad boss when they see what a positive attitude you always have. Or maybe God has you in that position so other coworkers will see the peace you have even while dealing with that bad boss, and they may want to know more about your faith and where you find that peace.

I confess I did not always demonstrate such a positive attitude, and I deeply regret that today. I encourage you not to make that mistake and to keep that in mind so that when you look back over your own career, you don't have that hollow feeling in your gut as you reflect back on some of your own failures to be a servant leader.

Every leader will have to give an account of how they served in the leadership role God placed them in. We are to obey our leaders and submit to them and trust God that He is in control, not our difficult boss. It is not up to us to have our boss fired or to whine and complain about our difficult boss. We are to leave that situation to God to deal with them, and we are to serve our boss in the best way we can, even if we have difficulty respecting them at times. We need to look at them as people God has made and remember we are far from perfect ourselves. God still wants us to obey them and to do our best to help make them successful as long as God wants us there.

But that doesn't mean we have to endure a difficult boss forever. Deciding when the right time is to leave a job can be a stressful time in your career. I can't tell you when it is long enough for you and when the right time is for you to leave a difficult boss or a job you can't stand. However, one caveat I would add is this: if you are in a position where you feel physically threatened, you should seriously consider leaving and seek employment elsewhere.

I always felt a nudge from God when it was time for me to move on. Even though I experienced my share of difficult bosses, I was fortunate during my career that I never felt things were so bad that I needed to leave a job because of a difficult boss. Sometimes I got to the point where I felt our team had accomplished what we had been hired to do and others on the team were ready to step up and take the team to a higher level.

Sometimes it was just a matter of feeling like I needed a new challenge, something to reenergize me so I would not fall into the trap of complacency. When I started to have those feelings, I prayed for God to give me discernment and for His will to be done, no matter what I was feeling. For me it was about every ten years or so. It will be different for other people.

Each and every time, through lots of prayer, I saw God opening certain doors and closing other doors to help me with my discernment. God wants all of us to be working, and I don't think He delights in watching us be miserable in a job, or flounder in our job wondering if we should stay or leave, or getting comfortable and complacent in a job we have been in too long. If you seek His will through prayer and even fasting, it is my experience that He will lead you where He wants you to be.

Pray to God for guidance and wisdom. But also know God has a plan, and He may have you in that situation to help you mature in your own faith and grow closer to God, or He may have you there to work through you to have an impact on others. Trust in God, and pray for wisdom. Remember, Jesus promised He would be with us always (Matthew 28:20).

We are each called to do the best job we can in any role God places us in and to allow the Holy Spirit to work in us and through us to bring success to the team and to the leader we are working for, regardless of our discovery that our boss is not perfect. We don't deserve any of the blessings God has given to us freely, so it our job to do our best to help our team and our boss succeed, continually seeking the will of God, and to reflect God to others in everything we do until God moves us to the next position He has for us.

And when it is time to leave, we should endeavor to leave well, not burn any bridges we may want to return to later, and hopefully leave with the respect and admiration of our team. None of us is perfect, and none of us can please everyone. But if we have done a good job staying focused on and consistently using the CLEAN principles, then when it is time to leave, we will have a better chance of leaving with the admiration and respect of our teammates, some sadness in knowing we will never be that close to them again, and hopefully the opportunity to continue to engage with them in the years to come.

*"For God so loved the world that he gave
his one and only Son, that whoever believes
in him shall not perish but have eternal life."*

JOHN 3:16

*"If you declare with your mouth,
'Jesus is Lord,' and believe in your heart that God
raised him from the dead, you will be saved."*

ROMANS 10:9

CHAPTER 11

The Ultimate Undercover Boss
Concluding Remarks

I TOLD you at the beginning of the book I would show you where the Bible talks about the Undercover Boss. I don't want to take this too far, but in a way King Jesus is the ultimate Undercover Boss!

We know Jesus is part of the Triune God of the universe, yet Jesus was humble when He came to live on this earth as a man, a simple carpenter. He had personal relationships with people many considered to be lowly. He showed us how to love others. Jesus lived a perfect life without sin and experienced what it was like to live on this earth. His life and His words recorded in the Bible have provided us with the model and the instructions on how to live our life as a servant of others. Jesus loves us and understands what we go through. He has been here, done it.

Jesus is our all-powerful Lord, God, and King. Yet Luke 2:7 tells us Jesus was born in a stable and was placed in a feeding trough—a humble birth. Jesus also chose to ride into Jerusalem on a donkey (John 12:14) just before going to the cross, a humble entrance considering He is God and Lord.

While this fulfilled the prophecy of Zechariah 9:9 given hundreds of years before, Jesus also showed His humility and how loving and humble He was as a leader.

He loved us so much, He took on the debt of our sins and died a horrible death on the cross to pay that debt for us because there was no way we could deal with our sin problem by ourselves. Through God's amazing grace Jesus did this for us—He did this for me, a messed-up sinner.

I grew up in a devout Catholic family with a loving mother and father. We never missed church on Sunday. I remember going to confession to confess my sins to the priest before church every Sunday, only to be back the following Sunday and going to confession again to confess all my sins from the previous week. That seemed like a never-ending cycle to me. I was worried I would never be able to get right with God on my own or by my own works. I knew I was a sinner who was falling far short of God's standards. As hard as I tried, I could never be good enough to make it to heaven.

Then, when I was thirteen years old, I joined a Protestant youth group and went on a youth retreat with them at the invitation of a close friend of the family (a person who served as my spiritual mentor for many years and I will always be grateful to him). On that retreat I learned that God wanted a personal relationship with me, not me trying to be religious to earn my salvation.

God loved us so much that through His grace He sent His Son Jesus to die for my sins in my place and to pay the debt for my sins. Jesus was crucified, died, buried, and then He rose again from the dead to prove He was God. His sacrifice to pay for our sins was acceptable to God the Father.

I learned that by placing my faith in Jesus Christ, my sins (past, present, and future) are forgiven, and I am assured of eternal life with Him. I learned that God understood our sin problem that was separating us from Him, and this was God's plan to deal with our sin once and for all.

God was offering to me, and to all of us as sinners, a free gift that I didn't earn and I don't deserve. I have nothing to contribute except my need for God's grace. On that youth group retreat, I placed my faith in Jesus Christ as my Lord and Savior and asked Him to send the Holy Spirit to come and live in me, to begin to change me so I could begin to live my life the way God intended.

I want you to know that placing my faith in Jesus Christ has brought me tremendous peace, joy, and contentment in my life. I am not perfect, and I still have struggles. But knowing God has adopted me as His child, and promises never to leave me, has brought tremendous peace to my life. No matter what I am going through, knowing how much God loves me, that my sins are forgiven, that I am assured of eternal life with Him, and how much He has blessed my life, makes me content. It definitely keeps things in perspective for me.

I don't think I could have made it through the most difficult trial of my life, the shipwreck with Linley, had it not been for my faith in Jesus Christ to give me the strength to get me through. Not only did He get me through, but what He taught me through that trial has been a life changer for me.

Because I have gotten to know Jesus and have a personal relationship with Him, I have come to understand how important it is to be a servant leader. Jesus is the model of servant leadership that we should all follow, no matter what our position is at work. I doubt we will be asked to die for anyone else the way Jesus did for us, but we should strive to live our lives as servants of and in love of others in every one of our relationships. We should let God be our leader. That is servant leadership!

Jesus not only taught us about servant leadership; He actually lived His life on this earth as a servant to others. He wants all of to follow His model and put our trust in Him rather than putting our faith in our own abilities to be leaders. He wants us to focus on helping others and putting them ahead of ourselves rather than always thinking about ourselves and our own plan. If we keep our focus on Jesus and ask for the power of the Holy Spirit to work in us and through us, we can live our lives as servant leaders and bring glory to God, as others see and know that we are Christians by the love and empathy we show to others.

As I said earlier, I believe most people show up for work wanting to do a good job. If you as their leader explain clearly what is expected of them, how they can contribute to the success of the team, and live servant leadership by demonstrating the CLEAN qualities (*commitment, listening, empathy, accountability, and notice*), I believe you are going to have a powerful team. It will be a place where everyone will want to give their best and contribute to the team's success.

I recommend you give it a try. Who wouldn't want to work for a leader and a company where everyone is truly committed to one another and the success of the team, listens to one another, shows empathy to and empowers everyone to give their best, where everyone is accountable to one another and gives notice to one another to show their appreciation. That is the model Jesus gave us.

I have not always been great at being a servant leader, and I have fallen short many times throughout my career to serve others as a servant leader. But what I can tell you is my life has been truly blessed when I get out of the way and allow God to use me as a servant leader as part of His plan in all my relationships.

God has blessed my life far beyond what I could have ever even dreamed. God has given me my loving, supportive, and beautiful wife, who is my best friend. She is the best gift God has given me outside of His Son Jesus Christ. I can't imagine life without her. She has always been there to give me support when I was going through difficult times. My wife has always been able to sense when I was under stress, and she has reminded me to turn control back over to God. She has prayed for me and with me. She brightens my day, every day! And when I look at the selfless devotion she has given to me, my daughter and my son, I know God will have a special place for her in heaven.

I know we can't earn our salvation from God, and our salvation is by God's grace alone, through our faith alone, in Jesus Christ alone (Ephesians 2:8–9). But trust me, if Dare has been able to stand by my side with her constant unconditional love and support me for the last thirty-nine plus years, she has surely earned some treasure in heaven!

And when I think of the blessing of my daughter, who is always excited to see me, and loves to Facetime me over twenty times a day—who else has a thirty-six-year-old daughter who still wants to talk to her dad that much? What a blessing and inspiration she is to me!

And then my pride and my namesake, my son, Larry IV. I did have some concern when my wife became pregnant again after the shipwreck with Linley that we might have another catastrophe. My son has brought immense joy to my life, watching him excel at baseball, getting to race sailboats and water surfing with him, hunting with him, and watching him mature into such an empathetic and respected man, full of integrity.

To see him now begin to excel and climb the leadership ladder in his business as a geologist, and to hear people I know who have conducted business with him tell me what a fine, hardworking, dedicated, knowledgeable, and honest man he is—I am proud of him. And now he has brought his beautiful wife, Christina, into our family whom we absolutely love. All our lives have been truly blessed by God.

Yes, God has blessed my life. I could not make it through life without knowing that God is with me always. Through His tremendous grace, which I don't deserve and can't earn, He has given me more than I could ever have imagined.

I am not saying that by striving to be a servant leader in all my relationships I am trying to place myself as *the leader* and in authority in all my relationships. Servant leadership works even when others are in authority over you. Remember how Jesus took His instruction from God the Father! Servant leadership is about me striving to be the servant to all the people I interact with or have relationships with—spouse, family, friends, and colleagues—and allowing God to be the leader and lead me! I pray each day for the Holy Spirit to remind me to be the servant and to help me trust God as my leader. Servant leadership!

I hope you will reflect on how you can better live your life according to Jesus' model of servant leadership at work, at home, and in all your relationships. God as leader, we as servants, and having people know we are Christians by the love and empathy we show others! Having God living inside you as a Christian and yet not accessing Him and turning control over to Him is the ultimate *management waste*. Without the right management in your life (God), you end up with *management waste*—a life lived apart from God's power to work in you and through you to serve and love others and bring God glory.

It is *management waste* to carry the burden of your own trash in your life and not to lay it at the foot of the cross and turn it over to God. You end up with *management waste*—a life of failure lived by your own power trying to work your own plan rather than letting God help you begin to use the CLEAN principles to clean up your life, haul off your trash, and trust in God and God's plan. Trying to live life with your sins and relying on your own power, and not walking with God, is a total waste. Put your sins, your ego, and your plans at the foot of the cross and trust God.

The Bible tells us:

- "For God so loved the world that he gave his one and only Son, that whoever believes in him shall not perish but have eternal life" (John 3:16).

- "For I am convinced that neither death nor life, neither angels nor demons, neither the present nor the future, nor any powers, neither height nor depth, nor anything else in all creation, will be able to separate us from the love of God that is in Christ Jesus our Lord" (Romans 8:38–39).
- "If you declare with your mouth, 'Jesus is Lord,' and believe in your heart that God raised him from the dead, you will be saved. For it is with your heart that you believe and are justified, and it is with your mouth that you profess your faith and are saved" (Romans 10:9–10).

If you have not yet placed your faith in Jesus Christ, but today you hear Him knocking on your heart, you need only to bow your head and pray to God:

> Lord, I know I am a sinner, and I know I am lost without You. I need Your forgiveness. I know You can take me and all my past mess-ups and turn my life into something good. I believe You sent Your Son Jesus, who came and lived a perfect life on this earth, died on the cross to pay for my sins, was buried and rose on the third day. God, I need forgiveness because I see I am lost without You. I receive Your gracious gift of eternal life and the forgiveness of my sins, which were bought and paid for by Jesus Christ, Your

Son, in whom I have placed my faith. I ask You to come live in me and through me. Thank You for Your unmerited grace and love toward me. I pray You send the Holy Spirit to live in me and to begin to work in my life to change my heart, and to change me so I can make a difference in the world around me. Help me bring glory to You, Father, in the way I act and the words I use at work and with my family and friends. And I pray this in the name of Jesus Christ, Your Son, our Lord and Savior. Amen.

If you pray that prayer, please reach out to someone you know who is a Christian and tell them you have become a Christian. Ask them to help you find a church to attend and to become involved with. And when you find a church you are comfortable with, please let the pastor there know you recently became a Christian and would like to be baptized. Then ask the pastor to help you find a mentor who can help you learn to pray, read your Bible, and begin to grow in your relationship with God.

I would love to hear from you if you pray that prayer. Please drop me a note at larry@larryodonnell.com so I can pray for you.

God wants each of us to live as servant leaders. Regardless of what you have been in the past, throw it into the trash, and let Jesus CLEAN you up so you can begin to experience the joy and contentment God's plan can provide. You just have to trust Him. Yesterday is behind you. The question is,

What kind of leader will you be today and tomorrow? How do you want people to remember you? What legacy will you leave behind?

As you consider how you might apply what has been presented in this book to your own life, I hope you will also see that these CLEAN principles can apply to all your relationships. Not just at work but also with your spouse, family, and friends. I pray that each of you reading this book will be inspired to CLEAN up your life and turn your life over to God. James, the half brother of Jesus, tells us to "draw near to God and He will draw near to you. Cleanse your hands, you sinners; and purify your heart" (James 4:8 NASB).

Ask God to remove your trash and help you seek His will for your life so you can begin to live your life the way Jesus modeled for us, humbly loving others and being a servant leader—serving others with God as your leader.

Scripture Index

Larry
O'Donnell III
Bio

LARRY O'DONNELL'S business career includes such titles as chairman of the board, president, and CEO, but he's probably best known as the first *Undercover Boss* from the CBS hit TV premier episode about Waste Management. A popular speaker, leadership consultant, and ministry leader, he holds a master's degree in Biblical and Theological Studies from Dallas Theological Seminary, and he leads businessmen and women around the world through his full-time ministry.

Larry has impacted countless individuals by serving in numerous leadership roles in some of the most success-ful companies in the country. An engineering major from the University of Texas, he also earned his J.D., cum laude, from the University of Houston, and practiced transactional law for nearly a decade before joining Baker Hughes, one of the largest oil and gas services companies in the world. After almost ten years at Baker Hughes, he became president and COO of Waste Management, where his transformative work earned him wide recognition, including becoming the first boss featured on the hit television series *Undercover Boss* on CBS in 2010.

After over ten years at Waste Management, Larry became a founder, CEO, and chairman of Rockwater Energy Solutions, a leading provider of water and chemical technologies for oil and gas completion, stimulation, hydraulic fracturing, and production, now part of a publicly traded company. During his tenure at Rockwater, he and his team received multiple awards, including Ernst & Young's Entrepreneur of the Year Award for the Gulf Coast and the Top Workplaces Leadership Award for a Midsized Employer by the *Houston Chronicle*.

As the founder and CEO of Servant Ministries Foundation, Larry's leadership training, speaking engagements, and mentorship/discipleship programs have helped thousands of servants become the leaders they were made to be. His weekly blog on faith and leadership, as well as his weekly podcast, can be accessed at www.larryodonnell.com and subscribed to by sending a text message to 56316 (JN316), typing "Larry" in the text message box, and hitting send.

He has held positions on numerous boards since 1995, but Larry's greatest joy is his family, which includes his wife of nearly forty years, Dare, as well as his special-needs daughter Linley, son Larry, and daughter-in-law Christina.

Website: www.larryodonnell.com

Facebook: www.facebook.com/Larry
            ODonnelliii/

Twitter: @larry_odonnell3

LinkedIn: www.linkedin.com/in/larry
            -o-donnell-44902510a.